DEDICATION

This book is dedicated to Muriel
my soul mate.
Fifty four years of wedded bliss
has been our fate.
She has been at my side with
intense loyalty;
Her support is so strong, I think I
am royalty

We have traveled through a long
life journey
In the harmony of solid
matrimony.
Good times we have had and some
of bad weather
,but no matter what the conditions,
we have done it together.

To write this book, I have learned
to converse
In the language of poetic verse.
I feel fortunate to have found
supportive publication
And I am proud to honor my wife
with dedication.

To: Jean & Ben,
Best regards!
Wilbur Shapiro
1/3/18

THE BAR-MITZVAH

Introduction

It happens to most Jewish boys of
thirteen.
This Bar-Mitzvah ritual, what does
it mean?
Some tell us, it's when a lad enters
maturity
,but we couldn't bank on that for
security.

It's a time when parents plan a big
celebration.
If they possibly could, they'd
invite the whole nation.
Why all this commotion, is it some
kind of ruse?
The whole affair tends to confuse.

Our ancient ancestors had good
reason.
A boy in those days much faster
did season.
Life was much shorter and less
complicated.
He knew of his future and how
he'd be situated.

There is inveterate meaning to this
Bar-Mitzvah condition,
From religious doctrine to long
standing tradition.

2

It's also a milestone in religious
education,
And stands at the threshold of
advanced preparation.

It's not a bad age to reflect and to
pause
On what will be his future life's
cause.
Environment and genes have had a
chance to develop,
Characteristics and talents indicate
directions to envelop.

Whatever significance, it's a time
of excitement.
When it arrives there's a climatic
enlightenment,
That our family and friends mean
so very much,
And that our son has grown up in a
terrible rush.

On the occasion, to our son we pay
tribute.
That he is king for a day no one
can refute.
His chanting and celebration will
indeed make us proud.
We thank the lord he gave us him
from the crowd.

The temple itself absorbs the hour
With a large pagoda like tower.

Our out of town guests were awed
with the sight.
The architect was Frank Lloyd
Wright.

Prelude

Through the mails the notice was
sent,
Concerning a future important
event.
It was vital that we not be late.
It seemed rather silly, since we had
a one year wait.

For Geoff's Bar-Mitzvah, a date
had come due.
It was scheduled for October 14,
1972.
To me the notice did not cause a
stir
,but there was an air of excitement
in her.

The wife wasn't one to be at all
hesitant.
That very weekend we saw the
Temple caterer resident.
No dilly-dallying, no playing a
hunch,
After the ceremony we'd have a
formal lunch.

Cocktails and hors-d'oeuvres for
an appetite teaser.

4

Then, Mushroom Barley Soup, and
a salad called Caesar.
The main course, a delicious beef
roast,
And with the meal, champagne for
a toast.

We wanted first class, the only
Bar-Mitzvah we'd make
,but I felt slight apprehension as
the caterer totaled the take.
With a nonchalant smile he glibly
said,
"This sweet kosher meal will cost
50 dollars a head"

Preparations continued for our
great celebration,
Next on the list came the
invitations.
Over 200 selected with
deliberation and reason.
Colors brown and yellow,
representative of the autumn
season.

The luncheon itself takes only a
very few hours
,but without decorations, the
atmosphere sours.
In the center of each table there
must be towers
Made of fragrant and very colorful
flowers.

The florist recommended a wheat
flower scheme,
To go with the fall seasonal theme.
He said "don't bother yourself, just
leave it to me".
At that time we considered it a
reasonable plea.

Sometime later, we saw a display
at another event.
The Missus loved it and set her
mind with a single intent.
Cancel our order and get rid of our
florist.
Order those we had seen that were
done by a purist.

Why is it that for a woman's every
whim and quirk,
It's up to the man to do the dirty
work?
Our florist was angry that we
disdained his horticulture.
We were lucky he settled for
deposit forfeiture.

The months ticked by too fast to
remember,
And here it was, almost September.
Invitations had gone, all seemed
very smooth.
We added dinner music for our
guests to soothe.

The star of the day prepared hard
for his role.
His part was augmented to read
from the scroll.
20 miles round trip to Temple,
three times a week.
We prayed his voice would not
change, and that he'd be at his
peak.

One would almost believe clothiers
did conspire,
To promote these affairs to sell
their attire.
New suits for the males ,but for
each only one.
For the females, gowns long and
short tripled the sum.

The RSVP's trickled in, they began
to return.
And with disappointment, we
surprisingly learned,
More refusals received than we had
anticipated.
Not many from friends ,but mostly
those related.

We limited distant relatives that we
could invite.
There was just too many and
discrimination would not be right.
You would expect our relations to
understand this plight.

,but never they do, only wrath did
we incite.

There was one of my aunts, whose
intellect is far from a sage.
Because of her uninvited
grandchildren went into a
vehement rage.
Yet her conduct was inconsistent, a
disparage,
Because for neither of her
daughters were we invited to their
marriage.

A respectful group affirmatively
replied.
Now a most difficult task that man
ever contrived,
Was to match this population
without causing estrangements,
Into congenial and stimulating
table seating arrangements.

We could not seat this cousin at
Table Number One,
Because his mother is there and
she doesn't talk to her son.
Also, try to combine commonality
of age or intellect,
,but be careful not to violate the
family hierarchy of respect.

A floor plan was made with tables
and names.

The options were varied like
detailed war games.
This delicate task caused
consternation and glum,
,but after much sweat and
consultation, the plan was finally
done.

To remember this time with more
than words to relate,
We decided upon a painted
photograph portrait.
Lights, action, camera, Geoffrey's
modeling de,but
Produced dozens of prints for
scrutiny and review.

The final selection, the one we
thought best of all,
Had Geoff smilingly brightly, with
blue suit, skull cap and shawl.
And now, several years later, it is
framed and stands tall,
As it hangs illuminated on the
living room wall.

To give our reception added
strength and vigor,
We went off to the State Store for a
large quantity of liquor.
Another customer there, a woman
hale and hearty,
After seeing what we purchased,
asked if she could come to our
party.

Many guests would come from far
away,
And we made reservations for a
place to stay.
A block of rooms was saved at a
nearby hotel.
We picked a wing that in comfort
they could rest for a spell.

,but our farsightedness would not
reign supreme.
For our guests were dislodged by a
visiting football team.
,but where they were placed,
though somewhat inferior.
Turned out much better than
appeared exterior.

Ceremony

The day had arrived, and we rose
early that morn.
We all hardly slept, such
anticipation was borne.
The men dressed in blue ,but of
modern décor.
Muriel in a knitted green gown,
draped not quite to the floor.

The service began at nine-thirty
direct.
To know who was there, I glanced
to inspect.

I don't usually separate ethnic
trends
,but the only ones on time were our
gentile friends.

The cantor sang out in his tenor
voice sweet.
For those unaccustomed, a rather
rare treat.
Although nothing new to our
observance dutiful,
This day the service seemed
extraordinarily beautiful

The time soon had come for
Geoffrey to sing.
My wife felt her heart, and
mentioned a ping.
I felt apprehension that his voice
would quake.
And I imagined that his knees did
severely shake.

,but he sang out aloud in glorious
soprano voice,
As if his rendition was his most
treasured choice.
The temple resounded with his
prayers clear and warm,
For this kosher ham really loved to
perform.

We knew he'd do well, we were
sure, we believed.

,but only after he started, the
tension relieved.
He had several parts, and never
once did he flaw.
He savored every last note right
through to the core.

The Rabbi's sermon projected into
future time.
For to be thou like Jacob,
omniscient and fine.
A bible and wine cup, the
congregation rendered.
After several swift hours the
services ended.

Luncheon

The festivities started with the
reception line.
"Greetings, Congratulations,
Geoffrey did so fine".
Then music, wine and cocktails
And enough hors d'oeuvres to
make anyone pale

Before the formal meal was served.
A reminder of rules to be observed.
For we were still in a Temple on a
Sabbath day,
At each plate, the observance was
related in the following way:

"Now that we've entered upon our
luncheon forum,

12

We must remind you of certain
Sabbath decorum.
Please don't eat too fast, we don't
want any choking,
And no matches are here, 'cause
there is to be no smoking"

"Dinner music allowed, by some
lucky chance,
,but hold back that urge to get up
and dance.
We hasten to add, we are at a
celebration and party,
So after the blessing is said, Bon-
Appetit, eat hearty"

Some could take those flowers
home.
And those were notified by poem.
"O lucky you to choose this seat.
Something extra to make the day
complete".

"After lunch is over, good things
don't cease.
We are proud to give you the
centerpiece.
To confirm that your winnings are
truth and not fable,
Please announce it to all who sit at
your table"

"Now that you are feeling so lucky
and grand,

You can take the flowers ,but leave
the stand!
If you're a man, there is a threat on
your life,
If you don't give those flowers to
your wife!"

At the luncheon, we avoided
platitudes and presentations.
For further formalities could
engender frustrations.
,but one congenial ceremony we
decided to make,
Was to light 13 candles on
Geoffrey's cake.

In prior preparation we created a
candle-lighting list.
,but as we kept on writing, we no
longer could persist.
For it was much too long to make
practical sense,
And we searched for ways to
condense.

It was impossible to take all
relations in account,
For this became an exorbitant
amount.
We stayed with Geoff's Uncles,
Aunts and cousins.
Eliminating parental relations,
whittled the number to proper one
plus a dozen.

The candle-lighting ceremony,
although trite, was cute
Of course, no feeling of ill was it
intended to impute.
Although we eliminated Auntie,
never did we dream what was
brewing,
For Auntie felt slighted, and she sat
fussing and stewing.

Pragmatic considerations decided
the course we had taken.
We intended no harm ,but we were
badly mistaken.
For Auntie's hatred could not be
any worse.
And she wished upon us a
perpetual curse.

In subsequent days we wrote to
apologize.
Her response was more of the
same, she accused us of lies.
Enough was enough, we finally
completely ignored.
With time she was lonesome, and
her friendship restored.

There is a lesson here, we cannot
deny.
In ceremonial honors, not all will
satisfy.
You'll end up accused of being a
person ingrate.

Our advice for that ceremony is to
eliminate.

Course after course with music
rhythmatic and sweet.
As hosts we circulated around for
our guests to greet.
We were proud of it all, pleasure
we could not conceal.
And we talked so much, we nearly
missed the whole meal.

Geoffrey, his friends and relations
his age,
Were at a great table in front that
was garnished with sage.
Impressive it was; they received
the most careful attention.
,but if each child ate half of his
food, it would be exaggerated
pretension.

Soon it was ended, after Roses,
Pom-Pom dessert,
And some brandy or cordial to
quench any leftover thirst.
Each guest and relation bid us a
fond personal farewell.
And the room emptied and quieted,
like the end of an oceans wave
swell.

Evening

Since our close families would stay
the weekend,
We felt obliged to host an
additional stipend.
For that evening we ordered fish
trays for a score.
We had cheese, bagels and lox
galore.

After completing a very heavy
luncheon,
In the evening what's desired is a
trifle to munch on.
So they just touched the food, and
ate only slight,
And we packaged food for the
freezer for half of the night.

With relief it was over, we felt no
longer taxed.
With close family and friends we
had a most pleasant evening to
relax.
Only Auntie was testy, reminding
us of what we did mishandle.
,but there was just no way she
could light that missed candle.

My brother Mickey decided to
leave about ten.
For his two sweet young daughters
fell asleep in the den.

17

He also took Mom and Dad and
Susan and her beau.
And Auntie and Uncle in their car
did follow.

Now Mickey's intelligent, a man
of clever perception.
,but his one major fault is his sense
of direction.
He hurried along with little
concern,
And went right by the street he
should have made a left turn.

Uncle obediently followed, the
mistake did not ring a bell
,but it seemed an awful long time
to reach the motel.
Some 50 miles in the country,
where the night air produced frost,
Uncle pulled alongside and asked
"Mickey you think maybe your
lost"?

After a long winded discussion,
they consulted a map.
They located the place where they
had made their lapse.
Some two hours later, they found
the motel at last.
And it was none too soon, for they
used their last drop of gas.

Conclusion

The next morning descended upon
us our brood,
To indulge in a little more of that
left-over food.
Another brother of mine who lived
close at hand,
Had us all to lunch to close the
weekend.

Then it came time for the family
farewell,
Back to all parts of the country
where they did dwell.
Fond embraces were made and
tears swelled in our eyes.
True bonds of kinship were once
again recognized.

The weekend weather was kind,
not a cloud marred the sky blue
distribution.
And the fresh autumn air smelled
sweet and free of pollution.
As the leaves fall, and are reborn in
Nature's refrain,
We will remember that time, again
and again.

FAMILY LORE

Introductions

Prior to presenting family
anecdotes,
Introductions are necessary so that
we may quote.
The father is Evan an impetuous
man.
He sired a pretty healthy clan.

Mother is Sylvia an intelligent
tactician.
With five siblings, at times she was
a magician.
The oldest was Anna, the most
intelligent.
She seemed to always know what
was relevant.

The oldest brother was Henry, who
cared not for school.
He was a hard worker and
nobody's fool.
The twins William and Alan were
six years behind.
They came next in the children's
line.

Last but not least came the
youngest Myron,
After thirteen years, quite a span.

In total that makes up the family
tree
Except for the dog whose name
was Frisky.

None of the stories are
psychological
Nor is the order necessarily
chronological.
There is no particular time span to
simulate;
The tales are happy memories for
the family to relate

The stories that follow could be
either fact or fiction.
They are told in a language of
poetic diction.
The author's intent is not to decoy
,but to give the reader a chance to
enjoy

Ice Cream

This story takes place a long time
ago.
Only two siblings existed for Evan
to show.
They were Anna and Henry, quite
young sister and brother.
They respected their Dad like no
other.

The time frame was during the
great depression.
Life wasn't easy; work was hard
with no concessions.
Evan had taken the children for a
walk.
He enjoyed this time for chatter
and talk.

They wandered by an enticing
candy store.
There were goodies inside galore.
Evan asked "How about some ice
cream?"
The children assented, "That would
be a dream".

For Anna and Henry, double scoop
cones.
They savored the treat in most
happy tones.
Evan also ordered a cone of
vanilla.

He smiled, no regrets, not one
scintilla.

Henry enjoyed the ice cream treat.
It happened seldom, it was really
neat.
Yet Henry was worried and
showed concern.
There was something from Dad he
had to learn.

"Dad for this treat, can you pay?"
"Money is tight, payment we
cannot defray".
Evan responded "We must
payment shun".
"When I give the word, both of
you run".

The children embarked as fast as
they could.
They ran hard and fast in the
neighborhood.
Meanwhile the proprietor opened
the till,
While Evan was smiling, he paid
the bill.

The Marble Fight

William and Alan were at age
seven
Identical twins, a gift from heaven.
They were inseparable with much
commonality,
Although, there was some variation
in personality.

One evening they were playing a
marble game
Where you shoot at a marble;
action was tame.
Tradition to them was a boring
bother
They could have much more fun
throwing at each other.

They didn't throw hard, what
counted was aim.
William was on target, Alan not
the same.
William was laughing at Alan's
ineptitude.
Alan's temper was rising, his
words not platitudes.

The contest continued, a one sided
affair.
Alan's emotions were rising, he
thought it unfair.
He calmly collected the marbles in
a nearby bag

And walked over to William
without any lag.

William looked up, "What's this
about?"
Then he knew and before he could
shout
The bag above his head so high
Came crashing down, "oh my, oh
my".

William was dazed, Alan satisfied.
Mother witnessed the scene and
was mortified.
She grabbed Alan and stroked a
good whack.
"You can't get away with that
awful attack".

Alan went crying to his room for
detention.
William was dazed, out of
contention.
"No more marbles allowed",
Mother said.
And William forever had little
bumps in his head.

The Play

The twins, William and Alan were
5 years old.
School was beginning,
Kindergarten took hold.
Classes continued morning and
afternoon.
A tiresome load for the boys to
consume.

Individual class work, at that age,
defied retention.
Many group projects was the major
attention.
A project was brewing for a pre-
announced day.
The class was to participate in a
school play.

Class involvement was minor, so
young at that time.
They were to march into the
gymnasium and form facing lines.
Not a difficult chore for the young
lassies and lads.
Their eagerness showed, their
demeanor was glad.

Rehearsals went smooth, according
to plan.
Two lines were formed with
William facing Alan.
A significant item necessary for the
play

26

The class must wear costumes
made from paper mache'.

The costumes represented birds,
namely robins.
The class was admonished to stand
still, no bobbin.
"For if there is excessive moving
around
The delicate costumes would fall to
the ground".

The day of the play brought joyful
excitement
Further enhanced by teacher
incitement.
Each of the students waited in line
As costumes were carefully added,
one at a time.

The costume attachment was
finally finished,
And the teacher once again
admonished,
"When you are standing in line
keep perfectly still
Just say to yourself, "I will, I will".

"One other reminder" the teacher
did confide
"Remember to exit on the other
side".
The time had come, they marched
into the gym.

The glorious play was about to
begin.

William faced Alan and gave him a
glare.
Alan was fidgeting and ignored the
stare.
"Be still Alan or your costume will
drop".
"Shut up William, your words
must stop".

Sure enough it happened, Alan's
costume dropped to the floor.
The audience reacted, laughing
galore.
Alan started crying like never
before.
He feared certain punishment that
was in store.

While crying, Alan tried to exit a
way that was wrong.
He realized, and turned around and
took a path that was long.
The audience clapped in hysterical
glee.
They enjoyed Alan's show, it was
for free.

The next day William was
besieged by upper class mates.
"Was that you whose costume did
deflate?"
"No, I want to tell you like so
many others
That boy who was crying was my
twin brother".

Popeye

The young twins, William and
Alan were told to prepare.
They were not sure why ,but they
were going somewhere.
They dressed in their best Sabbath
clothes
And awaited instructions, reasons
not disclosed.

Cousin Jason volunteered to
provide transportation.
The twins still did not know the
ultimate destination.
Mother and Jason sat in front of the
coupe',
The twins in the open air rumble
seat during the hospital foray.

At the hospital, the twins were
ordered to peel.
They looked astonished, is this
excursion real?
Hospital gowns went over their
skin.
The gowns reached the floor,
covering shins.

A nurse entered the room, her face
with a smile.
"Who wants to see Popeye?" she
asked with cunning guile.
After consistent persuasion, Alan
finally agreed.
William was leery; he did not want
to concede.

A nurse grabbed Williams hand
and led him along.
"I don't want to see Popeye", his
crying song.
The twins were laid on a hospital
table as they continued to blubber.
They were shown a Popeye doll
made out of rubber.

The next morn the boys awakened
in a hospital room.
Mother's cot between them to
soften the gloom.
"Mother, why are we here, the
boys did pout?
"You are here because it was time
to take your tonsils out."

A nurse came by with a gift of ice
cream.
This isn't so bad, although not a
dream.
The boys scooped up the cream
and what was next to follow
Was to savor the cream ,but it sure
hurt to swallow.

They rested that day because they
were tired.
They slept long and deep and
Mother stayed with what she had
sired.
The adventure was over,
satisfactory, complete
And Jason drove the boys home in
the rumble seat.

Soap Transport

The twins, William and Alan went
to summer camp when they were
pre-teenagers.
They enjoyed camp and the various
activities; camp became
contagious.
At various times, family was
entertained for purposes of liaison.
The visits were meant to show off
camp amenities for promotional
reasons

During one visit, it was the
afternoon hours
When Daddy Evans announced "It
was time for showers".
He took the boys to the community
bath house.
"The showers will get us clean
with a good water douse".

Daddy Evans and the boys
discarded clothes and stripped.
The wooden floor was wet so they
had to be careful not to slip.
Unbeknown to them, someone left
a cake of soap on the floor.
If you stepped on it and slipped
you could become very very sore.

As William prepared to step into
the stall
He stepped on that cake of soap
,but did not fall.
The slippery floor propelled him
rapidly across the floor
Some 30 feet away he headed for
the door.

William did not react and glided
effortlessly.
Most would try to dismount and
operate cautiously.
It seemed that William was in a
transport trance.
He was like a champion figure
skater ready to dance.

He traveled at least 30 feet without
a bend in his stance.
It was amazing to witness his near
perfect balance.
The soap met increased friction as
it progressed near the door
And William dismounted
nonchalantly and was ready to
proceed as before.

Daddy Evan questioned whether
William was all right.
He could not believe that soap
transport sight.
William said he was fine and was
ready to continue.
Daddy Evan chuckled, "Let's get
to that shower venue".

So what can we take from this
shower adventure.
Nothing much except William's
dementia.
Perhaps a lesson about bodies in
friction.
However, no need to consider a
soap transport addiction.

Uncle Nat's Spats

Spats were fashionable a long time
ago.
Their practicality was
questionable, they were primarily
for show.
They covered the shoe laces and
extended to the toe root.
Supposedly to enhance appearance
of a man's foot.

Uncle Nat was a brilliant executive
Unassuming and a wonderful
relative.
He dressed with fine suits of
sophistication
And spats were on his shoes; he
had no hesitation.

The young twins looked forward to
his visitations.
They would tear into his spats
without reservations.
Spats became untied at the blink of
an eye.
Uncle Nat would beam; he enjoyed
the execution without outcry.

At the end of the visit Goodbyes
were in mention.
,but wait, something was missing
that created tension.
Uncle Nat's right shoe spat was no
longer attached.
A search was initiated with hurried
dispatch.

They looked everywhere ,but that
spat could not be found.
It had to be somewhere, it must be
around.
It was getting late, the visitors must
leave.
That poor lost spat ,but no time to
bereave.

Several days later occurred a
surprising sight.
The neighbor's cat Tabby ascended
in the light.
She was small in stature ,but
exceedingly daring.
And on top of her coat a spat she
was wearing.

Tabby paraded around she was not
a shy cat.
And she looked quite Queenly
wearing that spat.
Now how did Tabby get that spat
to show?
For these many years, nobody
knows, nobody knows.

The Bicycle

On Saturday, the twins usually
went to the picture show.
They walked to the Sunnyside
Theater with anticipation all aglow.
They would see a movie, a serial
chapter, the Pathe news and enjoy
an intermission when prizes were
awarded.
They looked forward to Saturday
movies, they felt rewarded.

It was Saturday and movie time
was on their plate.
William's sinus acted up, so he
was to stay home and recuperate.
Alan and friend Jimmy to the
theater they were going.
The main attraction was a cowboy
western that was showing.

Alan and Jimmy enjoyed the
motion pictures.
Pathe news, Captain Marvel serial
and John Wayne with cowboy
fixtures.
The pictures shut down and the
lights illuminated for intermission.
It was game time for the lottery
decision.

Each attendee was given an
additional ticket with number.
A time of rapt attention, no time
for slumber.
A winning ticket could lead to a
pleasant surprise.
For the winner received a very
useful prize.

Alan was seated with his feet on
the seat back ahead.
He considered his chances of
winning all but dead.
He followed the numbers as they
were distinctly announced.
By golly, he had the right 5
numbers that were pronounced.

There were four winners called up
to the stage.
They were met by the emcee; he
courteously engaged.
Each was directed to select from a
hat that contained slips in a thicket.
For amongst those was the winning
ticket.

Alan was last to make his
selection.
To his pleasant surprise, a bike was
headed in his direction.
It was a 26 inch two wheeler
Rollfast beauty.
He was astounded ,but now to take
it home was his duty.

Alan and Jimmy wheeled that bike
home with dutiful care.
There was good news to spread
and for everyone to share.
When they arrived at the apartment
they yelled up to the window
"Alan won the bicycle"; the boys
had it in tow.

Older brother Henry went to the
window when he heard the noise.
"Just hold that bike where it is", he
ordered without much poise.
When he descended to the ground
he said "I'll take that bike".
Alan did not resist, after all he was
somewhat of a little tyke.

Alan did not know how to deal
with Henry's mettle.
He was young and probably could
not have reached the pedals.
,but still the manner in which
Henry did abscond
Was not kindly and more
protection should have been found.

Henry took advantage of his
younger brother.
Alan accepted and never
mentioned the appropriation to any
other.
And Henry for many years did not
have to hike.
As he rode into the sunset on
Alan's bike.

The Intercom

Evan Shaw was a salesman of
clever persuasion.
In business tactics, he was a
constant invasion.
He worked from his home with an
office in the basement.
A good living he made from this
convenient emplacement.

His wife Sylvia helped with
secretarial chores.
She typed and stenoed and did
filing labors.
Evan liked to be boss, he had a
nature categorical.
Many deals he had cooking, with
his manner rhetorical.

Now, Sylvia also had
housekeeping and cooking to be
done.
For Evan and Myron, a college
student and youngest son.
An idea struck Evan that would
enhance his aplomb.
Home communications could be
improved with an Intercom.

With transmitters in the kitchen
and in Myron's bedroom,
All of Evan's queries could be
answered without time to consume.
Evan spent that Sunday threading
the wire.
The thought of the using was all
that was needed to inspire.

Sylvia did not like the idea at all,
To be interrupted in the kitchen to
Evan's beckon call.
Myron was also not overly
delirious,
For he studied in his room, and he
did so quite serious.

All connections were made, it was
time for the test.
Anticipating fruitful rewards, Evan
was glad he did invest.
"Go upstairs Myron and turn on
your speaker.
I'll start out normally and
gradually speak weaker."

Now Myron was busy, he had a
test the next morn.
There was no time to play with
these toys of corn.
So in his bedroom, the speaker was
turned off.
He would not hear his father,
whether he spoke loud or soft.

"Can you hear me Myron, I have
the set turned on?"
I'll just wait a minute and give him
a chance to respond.
He waited for a time that seemed
eternally long.
"H'mm he did not seem to hear
me, what could be wrong?"

"Can you hear me Myron?" he said
with more vibrance.
,but again the same answer, a
noticeable silence.
He repeated again ,but this time
with more volume.
"Can you hear me Myron?" in
voice serious and solemn.

Soon he was screaming as loud as
he could.
Without amplification, he was
heard throughout the
neighborhood.
His neck veins protruded, he was
red, he was straining.
This electric contraption, his blood
was draining.

Finally, he quit, in a fit and a
cough.
Later he learned, Myron's set was
turned off.
The transmitters remained ,but
forever lied dormant.
And cobwebs gathered as on every
unattended ornament.

The Awning

He awakened the twins early in the
morning.
The day Daddy Evan decided to
install the awning.
He had purchased the cloth and the
metal supports.
They were American made and not
imports.

Without the slightest hesitation
The back porch was the
destination.
That's where the awning was to be
produced.
The shade will comfort, it was
deduced.

First a back wooden slab against
the wall of brick.
A ladder was necessary, no easy
trick.
No measurements were made, only
naked eye.
Evan was sure it was right, the first
try.

He pounded the slab with
penetrating nails
To install that piece to support the
rails.
The twins observed his actions, no
words to relate
Except when he yelled, "Is this
piece straight?"

Next, risers to the banister were
attached.
For that was where the top rails
were to be latched.
The labor thus far was difficult toil
Without proper tools brought his
temper to boil.

He thought there was daylight, the
end was near.
We hoped he was right, although
the boys had their fear.
The top rails were to go from the
back slab to the risers.
He felt confidence, no one the
wiser.

The top rails were sized to a
predetermined plan.
From the back to front, they would
cover the span.
He placed one rail up, with his
ladder to support.
,but golly gee the rail came up at
least one foot short.

48

Oh gosh, worst fears were realized.
The installation was not correctly
sized.
Would Evan explode or make a
strategic retreat.
He did neither ,but quietly
conceded defeat.

He was given credit for the attempt
,but more skill is required, not just
intent.
The exercise provided more family
lore
And the back porch remained just
as before.

The Can Opener

The kitchen counter was getting
cluttered.
Some things had to be shuttered.
Sylvia needed the room to prepare
her dishes.
More space became her fervent
wishes.

What could go and be non-
essential.
An examination led to one utensil.
The can opener standing erect and
tall
Space could be saved if hung on
the wall.

She told husband Evan about her
idea.
He immediately connected to his
handyman career.
A location wall was selected, out
of the way
So that it would not interfere with
the normal work day.

Evan told son Henry with a scowl
"Go down the basement and get
the dowels".
They were to be used for screw
insertion.
The wood support would allow
rotation.

With a pencil, the hole spacing was
marked
To match the opener holes for a
drill to embark.
With a hand drill the wall holes
were made.
No more smooth wall façade.

Next the dowels were cut to length
inches of three.
An appropriate size for interference
free.
Evan pounded them in with great
determination.
Entrance was difficult with some
reverberation.

Evan was stubborn, no one knew
better
He knew the procedure down to
the letter
Henry thought this installation was
folly
Instead of dowels, "What's wrong
with Moly's?"

Henry held the opener for screw
insertion.
Evan turned those screws with
great exertion.
At last, the opener on the wall was
situated
And the installation was finally
terminated.

A can was selected for the initial
test.
The cord was plugged in at Evan's
request.
The switch was turned on, and
Evan suddenly did frown.
When part of the installation wall
came down.

The opener is back in its counter
position.
To try to hang it again would be
sedition.
What's more important to family
all
Was how to cover that hole in the
wall.

Anna

The oldest was Anna, a wonderful
woman.
The only female of the clan, a
difficult omen.
Her four brothers were teasers, she
had to endure.
She handled it well, her confidence
secure.

She asked brother Henry to mail a
letter and purchase a stamp.
A simple request, no need to
revamp.
Henry marched out to the letter
box dome.
He mailed the letter ,but the stamp
he brought home.

The brothers soon reduced their
tricks.
Anna knew when they tried to be
slick.
Their conniving she could sense
and detect.
The boys soon offered nothing but
respect.

Anna went on to fashion design.
She had great talent and an
exceptional mind.
The brothers all were in awe of
their sister.
To them she never lost her
charisma.

Buster

Buster was a family dog offspring.
He was not a pedigree sibling.
He wasn't always well behaved to
put it mild.
In many respects Buster was wild.

The family erected a picket fence
in the yard in the back.
This was to contain Buster
although he had some slack.
,but Buster didn't accept the
containment.
He soon scaled that fence to search
for entertainment.

After he returned from his outside
adventure
He ran and leaped at the back door
enclosure.
The noise let the family know he
was home.
He was let inside, no more to roam.

On one occasion he traveled very
fast
And went through the storm door
with a glass blast.
He cut his leg up pretty badly.
A dumb dog, it was said sadly.

He recovered after a convalescent
session.
And it was hoped he had learned
his lesson.
Afterwards he continued his
prowling.
Although he caused the Chow
down the block to produce
growling.

Buster was a dog that was
inherently smart
Although his antics would deny the
part.
On one occasion Anna's fiancé
was sitting on the couch
And buster thought his leg a
hydrant, ouch.

When Myron was born, Buster
became a protector.
That baby was safe from any law
defector.
When Myron's nursemaid took
him for a walk
Buster would follow, he did stalk.

No dogs were allowed on the
shoreline boardwalk
,but buster followed the carriage,
he did not balk.
"Is that your dog", the policeman
pondered.
"No, he's not mine", the nursemaid
responded.

Another time, buster was walking
peaceful.
The boy's took him out and all was
gleeful.
Buster spotted Evan approaching
in the distance.
To greet his master, buster ran
without resistance.

He leaped on Evan, his method of
calling
And Evan went down on the
ground sprawling.
He was a difficult dog with certain
high qualities
He will be remembered with
storied jovialities.

The Sales Trip

Daddy Evan had to make a sales
excursion
Something to do with a cabinet
conversion.
He took Alan along to help with
the driving.
Some time the next day, they
would be arriving.

The trip was long and tedious,
enough to chagrin.
They finally stopped for the night
at a roadside inn.
The room was OK with closet,
desk and twin beds.
Ample resting tonight would
produce clear heads.

They had dinner that night at a
local eating place.
Alan thought it was nice, it was
quiet, it was solace.
They returned to the inn to prepare
for the night.
Each showered, watched TV and
finally turned out the light.

Evan got under the covers and
closed his eyes,
,but a noise was heard to his
surprise.
It was a moan and a groan coming
through the walls.
It sounded like horses in their
stalls.

Evan got up and started pacing the
room.
Alan awakened with a premonition
of gloom.
"Don't you hear that noise, it is
driving me crazy
If we don't get some sleep,
tomorrow will be hazy".

"That guy next door must be sick
and ill
He sounds terrible; he can't be
cured with a pill".
"I'm calling the front desk, he
needs medical attention
"I'll describe the problem, in total I
will mention".

Hotel security awakened the guy
and told of his noise.
He got up in a start and almost lost
his poise.
"I'm OK, there is nothing wrong
with my health,
I sometimes snore loud, a problem
with my breath".

Evan thought he was sick and
apologized.
He had no intention to deride.
He retired once more, without the
noise next door,
,but Alan slept restlessly as he
heard Evan snore.

Colloquialism

William served on a Carrier during
the Korean War.
The war was winding down, so live
action was not in store.
Rigorous training was the Navy's
option.
Continuous flight maneuvers was
the selected adoption.

One of the ship's ports was
Yokosuka Japan.
A naval base for repair and
maintenance according to plan.
On one such occasion, the
engineering officers had liberty.
And 5 selected to explore Japanese
society.

The five were William, Red,
Chuck, Gabe and Benjamin.
They rented motor scooters, each
with two cycle engines.
They traveled the Japanese roads
obeying the traffic rules.
They all did well without the
benefit of school.

After an hour or so, a break was
the decision.
They rested at a café, refreshment
they did envision.
William ordered a vanilla sundae
rather than a brew.
Red thought that sounded good and
said 'Make it two".

Chuck also liked the idea and
uttered "Make it three".
"Make it four", Gabe said to
maintain harmony.
Benjamin thought, "What the heck,
Make it five".
They were thirsty and hungry and a
sundae would thrive.

The waitress did her best to avoid
confusion.
The orders were clear; there should
not have been delusion.
When William's sundae came he
savored the cream.
,but Red was given two sundaes;
this was somewhat extreme.

Chuck was given three sundaes in
disbelief
And Gabe had four, this was pure
grief.
Benjamin topped them all with the
jackpot.
He was given 5 sundaes, which
was sure a lot.

The crew was shocked at the ice
cream inventory.
This surely was a comical story.
They all laughed heartily at the ice
cream situation.
It was beyond belief and
imagination.

The men shared all the sundaes and
the cost.
And they considered it worthy; the
sumptuous taste was not lost.
It was time to get on the scooters
and return to the Carrier.
,but they learned a lesson about the
language barrier.

Period!

Daddy Evan liked new
contraptions.
A dictating machine was the latest
attraction.
Dictation would enhance his
productivity.
The concept became a desirable
proclivity.

He opened the box and read the
directions.
It seemed rather simple and he
made the connections.
He installed in the proper slot the
cassette.
For which his words would be
inscribed without regret.

He unhooked the microphone and
began his dictation.
First he identified the receptor of
his dissertation.
"Letter to Irving Miller of Miller
Industries".
There were things to discuss,
various sundries.

"Now Irving, this is what must be
done"
Daddy dictated in a purely
conversational tone.
There was no thinking about
dictation formal.
It was if Irving was there and
speaking was normal.

The conversation went on for at
least fifteen minutes.
Continuous talking without any
limits.
Finally a breather after subjects
myriad.
Daddy remembered and finally
said "Period".

Now proper dictation requires the
word after every sentence.
Otherwise the dictation is a
continuous mass without
coherence.
So Daddy's experiment may
increase productivity
,but not if the transcription runs to
infinity.

Pity the transcriber who must sort
it all out.
She must be ready to give up with
a shout.
Long after the conversation is
gone,
The sentence keeps running on and
on.

Wrestling

Daddy Evan was a competitive
sort.
He accepted every challenge with
"I can do it" retort.
The underdog always became his
favorite.
Especially obvious when he
watched wrestling at night.

Now wrestling to some supplies
contentment,
,but is it a sport or a form of
entertainment?
Muscular men throw each other
around.
They get slammed to the mat and
amazingly rebound.

Daddy Evan gloried in the
exhibition.
He loved when the good guy
applied retribution.
He could not contain his
excitement at a good guy surprise.
He alit from his chair and laughed
so hard he had tears in his eyes.

During one particular match, the
bad guy applied tremendous
mutilation.
Daddy Evan was in a state of
serious consternation.
Then, the living dead arose and the
good guy fought back.
Soon he was pounding the bad guy
without any slack.

Daddy Evan revived from his
saddened state.
"Go get him", he shouted "It's not
too late".
His excitement was building to a
feverous pitch.
"Hit that bad guy and send him to a
ditch".

Daddy was up and swinging his
arms
To pound that bad guy and do him
much harm.
Daddy swung so hard without
support to shore
That he tumbled and found himself
on the floor.

The fall caused some shoulder
pain.
So Daddy left to apply salve for his
strength to regain.
He could not watch what remained
of the match.
The bad guy won; at least Daddy's
disappointment wouldn't hatch.

The wrestling protagonists finished
the exhibition.
They left separately, both in good
condition.
The bad guy was booed by the fans
as he left for safe haven.
It's ironic that the only one hurt
was Daddy Evan.

Airline Tickets

Evan was scheduled to fly out at
three.
An important business meeting, he
had people to see.
When the time came for Evan to
leave,
Certain panic developed that sent
pangs up his sleeve.

The airline tickets were nowhere to
be found.
Evan was fitful; he may have to
stay on the ground.
He called the whole family
together
"Help find those tickets or else
there will be stormy weather".

Now Myron was young and not yet
speaking.
He was walking fine ,but his words
were squeaking.
He knew that his father was going
away.
He did not like that, he wanted him
to stay.

70

Anna surmised that there was
something fishy.
She suspected someone of being
tricky.
"Myron, where are the tickets,
Daddy needs them now".
The rest of the family looked at her
with a scowl.

"Why are you asking him", they
inquired
"What would he know about the
tickets desired?"
Anna insisted and pleaded with
Myron
"Daddy must leave on an airplane
to go on".

She continued her pleading and
crying lament.
Myron looked at her as if he knew
what she meant.
Then all of a sudden, Myron lifted
the bed cover.
He exposed the tickets that needed
recover.

The moral is there are none too
young
Who can do certain things if they
feel they've been stung.
Anna had the correct intuition
To bring this episode to fruition.

As for Myron he almost did cry.
It's like he was saying, "I'll give it
a try".
He kissed Daddy Evan and gave
him a hug.
Daddy Evan responded, his
heartstrings a tug.

The Grown-Up Suit

The family men awaited
downstairs
All dressed in suits for a relative's
affair.
Mother and Myron were upstairs
dressing.
The men watched TV, the news
they were digesting.

Myron was a tot of age about five.
He was lots of fun, on life he did
thrive.
The men were surprised when
Myron arrived.
He was dressed in new clothes,
beautifully contrived.

He wore a tweed sport jacket, color
light blue.
His pants were dark blue to
provide a contrasting hue.
A button down white shirt showed
through his sport coat,
And a polka dot bow tie covered
his throat

Argyle socks and new brown shoes
completed the attire.
Myron felt ecstatic, his brain was
on fire.
He felt he had been released from
the baby cult.
He now was a fully fledged adult.

Myron's appearance made the
spectators glad
As he strutted, he uttered "How ya
doin Dad?"
This little spectacle of innocent
consequence
Was remembered for a long time
and still has resonance.

Young Myron was a source of
infinite pleasure.
Since birth he became the family
treasure.
It is very enjoyable to witness a
sibling emerge from a pup.
It is just too bad we all grow up.

Frisky

Myron was the youngest of the
clan,
Thirteen years to the next at hand.
He had plenty attention ,but not of
his age.
How could he be more suitably
engaged?

Evan and Sylvia thought a plan
through.
"We'll get him a pup, that should
help do"
Off to the pond on a day somewhat
bitter
They picked out a pup, the cream
of the liter.

She had a coat like a collie ,but a
size much smaller.
"Myron was ecstatic, "What shall
we call her?"
She was jumping around, greeting
everyone she could.
"Frisky, fits for a name that sounds
good"

A friendlier dog, never could you
find,
Smart as a whip, a wonderful
mind.
She loved to be petted, and would
nestle her nose
To family members seated in
repose.

Evan often took her to the post
office so his mail was not late.
He picked out a spot for her to sit
and await.
She immediately obeyed without a
whimper or bark.
Instructing her was a most
pleasurable lark.

She was a wonderful pup,
appearance so elegant.
The family was surprised when
they found she was pregnant.
A litter of five came out rather
easily.
No difficult birth ,but not
necessarily measly.

She took care of those pups as if
royal breeding
Watching over them, and lying
down for breast feeding.
A wonderful mother with caring so
good.
When the pups were given to
friends, Frisky understood.

Her bearing remained she appeared
almost royal.
To the family she was exceedingly
loyal.
After a time, life was over, the end;
To the family, they lost not a pet,
they lost a friend

Lost at Home

Brother Henry served in the Army
during the Second World War.
He was in the Pacific with the
Army signal corp.
After the war Henry returned home
from battle strife.
He had to make an adjustment
back to civilian life.

The family lived on a street with a
string of attached homes.
The all had identical architecture;
they were clones.
The family home had one
distinguishing feature;
A fire hydrant in front was the
difference creature.

Henry wanted to visit old friends
from the past.
He took public transport; bus and
subway the last.
He thoroughly enjoyed the
acquaintance renewal.
The buddies all drank to their
future; friendship was their jewel.

Henry returned in late afternoon.
It was still daylight ,but you could
see the moon.
He entered the front door ,but the
commute made him frown;
He saw the couch and decided to
lie down.

Henry fell asleep and was soon
dreaming.
He was awakened suddenly by a
women screaming.
"What are you doing here,
invading this home?"
Henry was foggy, confused and his
appearance uncombed.

"Isn't this my home?" Henry
replied in a panicky state.
Then Mary realized who Henry
was and began to relate.
"Henry you scared me ,but you are
in the wrong place".
"You live down the block where
the hydrant does face".

Henry thought he was headed for
jail.
He wondered whether the family
would bail.
He never had a great sense of
direction,
,but this mistake was a serious
indiscretion.

And so Henry would never again
make the wrong house mistake.
The incident provided a strong
lesson to take.
He went on with his life in a
fashion quite vibrant,
And he never forgot the location of
the hydrant

Daddy, the Man

Daddy Evan was the patriarch of
the family clan.
It is time to ask "What kind of
man?"
Let us describe him in totality
To gain perspective of his
personality.

He was born at the turn of the
twentieth century
,but not to a family of wealthy
gentry.
Three sisters and a brother were
siblings.
He was the youngest, they had no
inkling.

Evan grew up in a New Jersey city.
It was where the weak had no pity.
He learned to fight hard for things
in need,
And he garnered self confidence,
he did not concede.

His education ended in high-
school,
And he became a contributor to the
work force pool.
He learned many trades; he was
quick and adept;
He flourished and was treated with
respect.

He played sand lot baseball, a
pitcher of renown.
A southpaw with a sizzling curve
known throughout the town.
He played for fun with no future
aspirations;
His primary objective was success
in the business nation.

During WW1, he enlisted in the
Navy.
He considered his duty an act of
bravery.
He was skinny and considerably
underweight.
He ate many bananas to pass
enlistment without debate.

His brother Henry became an
infantry soldier.
Trench warfare, nothing could be
bolder.
Against the Germans he fought
with energy to burn.
Unfortunately, a grenade did him
in; he did not return.

In the Navy, Evan was a telegraph
operator.
He learned Morse code as a dot-
dash translator.
He served aboard a Navy supply
ship,
And did his duty well on many sea
going trips

After WW1 he set out on a civilian
career.
He committed to civilian life
without any fear.
No particular objective crossed his
mind.
He was opportunistic and jumped
at whatever he could find.

His mindset was to work on his
own.
He did not seek a job that he could
bemoan.
The times were during the great
depression.
He labored with dedicated
obsession.

He wooed a woman with whom to
marry,
And they did so, no time to tarry.
Evan and Jeannette were the happy
couple.
A life of happiness awaited, no
signs of trouble.

They settled into a life of bliss;
God gave his blessing, they could
not miss
The family increased with Anna's
birth.
It was a time of celebration and
mirth.

One year later, son Henry emerged.
A close knit family was what
converged.
Evan worked hard to conquer the
depression.
Hard times would not cause
suppression.

Evan honed his entrepreneurial
skills
Through various enterprises
without many frills.
He produced lamps that required
extensive gumption,
And then sold them to retailers for
public consumption.

Some six years after Henry, the
twins came along.
The additions were welcomed to
the family they belonged.
William and Alan received plenty
of attention
From family, relatives and friends,
we must mention.

It was two years later that tragedy
struck.
The family retreated and ran out of
luck.
Mother Jeannette's diabetes caused
her to succumb.
She was only 32, and the death
made the family numb.

What was Daddy to do with 4
motherless children on his hands?
Lucky for him, his sisters could
help and take command.
Anna to Aunt Hilda, Henry to Aunt
Mary.
The twins needed a home, Daddy
could not tarry.

There was no choice, the twins
must be sent to foster care.
He worked hard to find a suitable
family with confidence they could
share.
He settled on a German family of
three,
Mother, Father and son whose
name was Henny.

The twins were destined for a two
year span.
Daddy wanted his family back that
was his plan.
Sylvia worked as a secretary in his
business foray.
They became a couple; Daddy
would recoup what was taken
away.

Daddy and Sylvia were engaged
and then wed.
He could now go back to being
family head.
They gathered Anna and Henry
from their Aunts,
And they set out to recover the
twins; they were parents.

It was a heartfelt day when Daddy
and Sylvia went to make the
recovery.
The twins were unknowing; to
them it was a discovery.
They were going to live with
Daddy and leave foster care
From the heart broken foster
family whose grief would long
time wear.

Daddy worked hard at his business
endeavors.
Life was a struggle and there were
no favors.
The depression had taken hold
making life difficult.
,but Daddy plowed ahead with a
survival result.

His vitality and creativity were
quite amazing.
He worked at his business
activities with effort blazing.
During WW2 he made products for
the Army's deficiencies.
He ran a big manufacturing plant
with excellent efficiency.

His taste for big business enhanced
his ambition.
Unfortunately, his dreams and
desires produced a negative
condition.
It's ironic, but true, success was his
undoing.
When he reached the top, bad
decisions was what he was
pursuing.

As time went on, health entered the
equation.
An enlarged heart not responsive to
sedation.
Before he reached 80 his condition
was grim,
And then finality came, he
contested ,but could not win.

His vitality and energy was truly
infectious
That only transmitted a kinship
feeling amorous.
He was beloved by family, there
was no refute.
To pay homage, they would all
stand at attention and salute.

Family Update

Some tales have been told ,but
what's the family's current state?
And so it's my duty to relate
The family cannot live on forever
No matter how we try or endeavor.

The first to go to god in heaven
Was the patriarch, daddy Evan.
Several years later Sylvia met her
maker.
She was the matriarch and god did
take her.

Brother Henry had heart problems
for a long time.
He did his best to stay healthy and
fine.
,but the pacemaker and
defrillabrator were not enough.
He finally succumbed, a loss that
was tough.

Anna had lost her husband Jack.
Her life became difficult, she could
not detract.
She had numerous health problems
that crimped her style.
She fought on hard and lived for a
while.

What was left of the storied family,
who lives?
William and Alan, the twins
survive.
The youngest brother Myron
continues on.
The three are all that is left of the
family clan.

What happens when there are no
more members?
Is there any way to remember?
Children are the only tether
,but that can't last forever.

How can anyone provide a lasting
legacy?
It is a difficult question for anyone
to see.
No family member has basked in
fame
So there is nothing for anyone to
remember the name.

,but that's not the reason we live
and die
Our lives are important when we
are alive.
To do our best to make things
better
And let the next generation become
our debtor.

The Honey Moon

William and Myrna in August were
married.
Off on a honeymoon, no time to
tarry.
The first night in an airport hotel.
The wedding was fine, they were
feeling swell.

The plans were to visit Anna, a
sister sibling.
Across country she lived, they
needed a wing.
The next day family and friends
met at the airport.
They all said "keep us informed,
we need your report".

There was one little catch about the
trip out west.
An obligation for the couple to do
their best.
This one was odd like no other,
Besides the married couple along
came the kid brother

However, the couple did not mind
the intrusion.
Myron was well liked and would
not cause confusion.
Now in those days, jets were an
imagination,
The propeller plane was a
Lockheed Constellation.

It only flew about ten thousand
feet.
For ten hours the ride was not
sweet.
Myrna had never flown before,
And after the wedding night the
couple was sore.

They all finally made the
destination.
It was nice to see the family's
relation.
There were Anna and husband
Steve;
The children Jean and Phil, they all
did receive.

Anna's idea for a gift to the couple
Was a trip to Las Vegas, it sounded
like trouble.
Anna and Jean were to get there by
plane,
The rest were to drive through the
desert flame.

The trip through the desert was
quite scary.
Temperature near one hundred can
make anyone leery.
There is a worry that the car can
overheat.
No civilization in sight makes the
heart skip a beat.

We finally arrived and met up with
Anna and Jean.
We quartered at a hotel that was
fairly clean.
The newlyweds planned to take out
the boys to keep them employed.
They searched the revues and
selected a show the children might
enjoy.

The show selected was to have a
proper star.
She sounded for children, her name
was Candy Bar.
The couple was shocked and
somewhat bitter
When they learned Candy Bar was
a noteworthy stripper.

Myron and Philip both smiled
galore.
They never saw anything like that
before.
Myron was staring, his glasses
were steaming,
Philip was happy his face beaming.

The newlyweds were in a state of
embarrassment.
That was not a show for children,
they felt harassment.
The boys told Anna and Steve of
their sights.
They went to bed smiling and
turned out the lights.

Anna and Steve took the couple
out for a show.
They thought that was nice ,but
they didn't know
On the stage came beautiful girls
flying down.
They were scantily clad, tanned in
Las Vegas brown.

William and Myrna were blushing
and troubled.
The show was not for a
honeymoon couple.
However, the couple admitted Las
Vegas was fun,
,but they were glad when it was all
done.

They all headed back to San
Francisco.
Myron flew back home ,but he
enjoyed the go.
The couple thanked all for an
exciting stay,
And they went on their way to visit
LA

The Volkswagen Bug

William's job in the city required a
commute.
He traveled by subway, the best
method without refute.
He attended classes at night several
days a week.
On those days he drove, for his
masters degree he did seek.

The drive to the city could be a
nightmare.
Most people drove as if they didn't
care.
William thought about a smaller
car
That would make life easier, by
far.

Then one day he dropped by a
dealer.
He looked Volkswagen bugs over
and put out a feeler.
He went out with a salesman and
took a test drive.
This was the car for the city, it
made him feel alive.

After he purchased the car, he
called Myrna his girl.
"I bought a new car, let's give it a
whirl".
"The car looks very cute" was her
initial remark.
"It's great for the city and so easy
to park".

One thing is true about any car
Without gas they can't go very far.
William was so excited he forgot
to fill the tank
They ran out of gas, their
enthusiasm sank.

William said "Don't worry there is
an emergency feature".
This Volksy was a well designed
creature.
"I just have to shift the lever on the
floor".
"Then we will have enough gas to
get to the gas station store".

The lever was flipped ,but the car
wouldn't start.
William was disappointed that the
car was not that smart.
The only way to get out of this
abysmal morass
Was to call brother Alan to bring
them some gas.

William had tried his best to brag
and impress,
,but he completely failed and did
much less.
Myrna was great and very
understanding.
She was taken home later without
demanding.

Later on William and Myrna did
wed.
They were glad their happiness
was fed.
One year later, pregnant she
became.
They both were ecstatic while they
thought of names.

The time had come for the hospital
ride.
William entered the Volks with
Myrna at his side.
It happened very late at night so
the traffic was bare.
That little car hurried to the city for
hospital care.

Myrna went in and she did scream.
,but out came Geoffrey, their
family dream.
William thanked the Volksy for
being A-number one
For getting them to the hospital for
the birth of their son.

The Garage Door

William and Myrna were married
ten years.
There were three including a son
they had reared.
They had recently purchased their
first home.
It was a split level, a nice layout to
roam.

William worked in the city, an
engineer by trade.
He worked hard with computers
and programs he made.
Myrna substituted in the local
school.
She taught the youngsters with a
skill that could rule.

They each had an auto and drove to
employment.
Life was busy, not much time for
enjoyment.
The new home had a garage for
two cars to store.
Each bay was enclosed by a
separate door.

One day Myrna was called
urgently to school.
She needed to hurry, no time to
fool.
What happened next was a comical
sight;
Myna opened the left garage door
and backed the car out the right.

William had difficulty to contain
his laughter.
He thought he had time to fix the
door after.
,but Myrna insisted that not be the
case
"Fix that door right away, I want
you to race".

You might think that's the end of
this tale.
There is more to tell and it's
laughable.
William divulged Myrna's
transgressions to a neighbor across
the street.
They laughed and William
admonished "Please don't repeat".

Then the neighbor had to digress.
He had something to tell, to
confess.
What he said really topped it all.
He drove his car in the garage right
through the den wall.

The Eye Test

William and Myrna moved to New
York State.
He was offered a better job, an
engineer's gait.
They found a home that was
attractive,
And they made the move without
anything subtractive.

As new residents they needed new
licenses to drive.
That's something required as soon
as you arrive.
The driving part was reciprocal
with the last state.
However, there was an eye test
requirement to stay up to date.

They both traveled down to the
Motor Vehicle Bureau.
They filled out the papers on the
line for eye review.
The testing machine was like a
microscope device.
You looked inside and read the
letters, sometimes twice..

William let Myrna advance in the
line.
He was in no hurry, he had plenty
of time.
Now it was Myrna's turn to test.
It should not be too hard if your
eyes had rest.

She looked through the viewer at a
very slow pace.
What could be wrong, does she
have a case?
She then said to the attendant
"Could you focus this thing".
If she could have read the chart, it
would have had a better ring.

When William heard Myrna's
words his face got red.
He was wishing he was somewhere
else instead.
Later on the incident gave him a
laugh
When he thought about his wife's
gaff.

She passed the eye test with her
glasses on,
And she had something to reflect
upon.
Whenever she drove she thought
about that test,
And she kept her glasses on to
avoid arrest.

The Basketball Court

William decided to build by the
driveway a basketball hoop.
At that time portables were not
available, that's the straight scoop.
The backboard with rim and net
came with a pole.
To install it you sealed it with
cement in a hole.

One weekend William took his
spade
To dig the hole in the lawn grade.
It was to be located at the driveway
rear edge
A good spot and clear of the hedge.

He took his spade and started to
dig.
"This should not be hard; it will be
up in a jig".
,but not so fast, his spade hit rock
To William, this was somewhat of
a shock.

The situation called for a different
approach
He thought about it ,but he didn't
have a coach.
There was one thing to do, he
could rent a jack hammer.
He could then pound down and
break those rocks with a slammer.

He proceeded to get the hammer
device.
It was electric no need to do the
job twice.
He pounded the rock with all his
might;
He was sweating profusely, not a
pretty sight.

After several hours of hammering
away
He broke up the rock in his best
way.
He then dug the hole sufficiently
deep.
It was hard work; he was tired and
wished he could sleep.

He inserted the pole and shimmed
it up vertical.
This job was hard ,but not exactly
surgical.
He mixed some cement and poured
it into the hole,
And he attached ropes and stakes
to prop up the pole.

He had to wait until the cement
dried tomorrow
So he returned the jack hammer he
borrowed.
He felt it had done its job.
He celebrated at dinner with corn
on the cob.

The next day the pole was rigid
and straight.
William thought to himself "this is
great".
He attached the backboard and rim.
And put on the net, he had his
gym.

He bounced the basketball and
took several shots.
He did pretty well, and he felt he
was hot.
So the basketball hoop was now
installed,
And William could practice, he
was enthralled.

The next day it was time to drive to
work.
William backed out of the garage
and there was a sudden jerk.
William said, "oh no, I backed into
the pole".
That basketball hoop was taking its
toll.

Now wherever that car went
The rear bumper had a big dent.
When asked how that dent
occurred
William shrugged shoulders, he
demurred.

The story is not over yet.
The punch line is coming you
won't forget.
A major storm was passing around,
And it laid the hoop assembly flat
on the ground.

Lost in the Station

For William and Myrna an
anniversary was near.
Time for a celebration after 25
years in the clear.
After work they would meet at the
train station.
Dinner and a movie would be their
celebration.

Myrna would take a commuter
train from home.
William could walk to the station
dome.
William left early so he could meet
the train.
This would save time, albeit a
small gain.

The train pulled in right on time.
William looked forward to a night
out sublime.
He met the train at the docking
platform,
And waited for Myrna to embark
for the evening's sojourn.

A crowd detrained and hurried
along.
William searched for Myrna ,but
there was something wrong.
As passengers emerged from the
train into the light
They hurried along ,but Myrna was
nowhere in sight.

Perhaps she slipped by William
without knowing.
He knew she would be dressed in
garments glowing.
She must have missed the train and
will take the next.
In the interim, William sat down to
read some text.

The next train was due in one hour;
William's mind set was getting
sour.
"How could she miss the train for
our date?"
William was an on-time freak and
hated to be late.

The next train arrived on time.
,but no sign of Myrna viewed from
the platform incline.
This was getting serious and
William felt an anxiety panic.
For Myrna could not be seen
through the pedestrian traffic.

William called a neighbor to
determine if Myrna had left.
He learned that Myrna had also
called; he was bereft.
At least he knew that she was
somewhere in the station.
He began a systematic search for
his spousal relation.

William sifted through the crowd
with eyes peering everywhere.
He was intent on his search with
laser like care.
Then it happened, behind a small
gathering he spotted Myrna who
was looking around.
William called to her, his prey he
had found.

Rather than cast blame, they both
waved off discussion.
Anxicty and panic were gone, there
would be no repercussions.
It was too late for dinner ,but the
movie they selected was not
chosen at random.
It seemed quite ironic that the
name of the movie was
"Abandon".

The Ladies Room

William and Myrna always were
together shopping;
From supermarket to department
store they were hopping.
,but no matter where they went to
buy
To the bathroom Myrna went while
William sighed.

Every time Myrna returned,
William was ready.
For Myrna had a tale to tell, the
stories were steady.
"There was no hook in the
bathroom stall".
"I would like to report it ,but who
do I call."

Or, "I couldn't lock the stall door,
"And I had to keep my jacket on
the floor".
Or, "I locked the stall door, and
could not get out".
"Lucky for me a nice lady heard
me shout".

Or "There was no toilet paper, I
had to use tissues".
Just another one of the bathroom
issues.
Or "They should have someone to
clean the place".
"Some people are sloppy and do
not have grace".

Or "The soap dispenser was
completely empty".
"I am sure they have a stock that is
plenty".
On long car drives, the situation
was the same.
"We must stop at the next
restaurant", a familiar refrain.

Wherever they go comes the
accustomed tune
Myrna must populate The Ladies
Room.
Presently, it's great to see women
ascend the success ladder,
If only God had given them a
bigger bladder.

The Winning Ticket

William and Myrna to Florida,
they took flight,
Where the weather is warm or hot,
day and night.
They went to see Sister Anna and
husband Jack.
For one week they would stay and
then fly back.

While they were there Anna made
a suggestion.
The beaches were crowded, too
much congestion.
She was not void of ideas, she did
not lack.
"Why don't we all go to the race
track?"

William agreed, he did not like to
ramble.
Secretly, he suspected, that Anna
liked to gamble.
Off they all went, not for good
causes.
Their objective today was to pick
the right horses.

The club house was comfortable,
nicely air-conditioned.
In the background, playing was
soft musical renditions.
Anna kept busy selecting her
stallions.
She was very good and deserved a
medallion.

On one particular race Anna
thought she had a sure winner.
She announced that her winnings
would pay for dinner.
William was skeptical and he bet
what he thought was hot;
To come in third, he bet on a long
shot.

While the race was in progress all
attention consumed,
Nature called William to the men's
room.
Anna's horse laid back and did not
come in.
They were all unhappy, a case of
chagrin.

Anna took her ticket and ripped it
apart.
Myrna followed suit, she thought it
was smart.
When William returned, Anna told
him," we lost".
"Not me, my long shot placed",
was William's retort.

Then William asked where his
winning ticket was.
No one answered, there was a
silent buzz.
Myrna finally responded with a
voice that was sad.
"I tore up your ticket, please don't
get mad".

William sat down in a terrible huff.
To lose a race you had won is very
tough.
Myrna was determined to right her
wrong.
She thought about what to do for a
time that was long.

Myrna picked up the pieces of the
torn ticket.
She sought an administrator from
the population thicket.
She showed him the pieces and
begged him to allow
The winnings to be paid, her
beseeching was not shallow.

They scotch taped the ticket in a
corner nook.
He allowed the payment, and
Myrna was off the hook.
There is a message here which says
"Aw Shucks!"
That stupid ticket was worth all of
five bucks.

Robin at the Window

In springtime the robins appear;
It seems they come from
everywhere.
They hop along the ground with
red breasts extended
Reminding one of their royalty
intended.

One morning we heard a noise at
the storm door.
A robin flew away when it was us
he saw.
Later on we heard the noise at the
bay window.
It was the robin, the window he
flew into.

The birds stake out their territory
and are very defensive.
Although what he was doing was
very offensive.
In the glass he saw his own
reflection.
He thought it was an invader that
needed deflection.

How can we stop the robin's
attacking?
What could we do, our ideas were
lacking?
He did a good job of dirtying the
glass.
That robin just did not have any
class.

We posted a cat's portrait to scare
him away.
,but just to another window he did
stray.
Down in the basement, the laundry
was sorted.
He attacked the basement window
it was reported.

This bird was causing us
nightmares.
He awakened us early, he didn't
care.
What could we do to find a
solution?
We would have loved to cause him
a contusion.

This sequence went on for several
weeks.
This bird must have been an
isolated freak.
Then one day all the noise did halt.
We knew not why, and what
caused the default.

Perhaps Mr. Robin found a female
partner.
We only hope she was a little
smarter.
He left us with plenty of windows
to clean,
,but at least we can enjoy the days
serene.

The Mailbox

Auntie and Uncle drove down to
visit their relations;
William and Myrna had made all
preparations.
And they anticipated that all would
be fine;
They all looked forward to a good
time.

The sleep couch was opened with
clean bedding installed,
And the conversation digressed to
many recalls.
William prepared steaks outside on
the grille.
They had plenty of food for their
stomachs to fill.

The guests rested comfortably on
the sleep couch.
They slept well, there was no
grouch.
It was quite comfortable with a
bathroom nearby.
All was going well everyone was
high.

They all had breakfast of eggs and
omelets
With toast and coffee, the food was
great.
,but Auntie and Uncle had to
embark.
They were anxious to get on the
road and be home before dark.

The visitors thanked their hosts and
started good byes.
They had a fine visit and Auntie
did cry.
The car was parked on the
driveway and they had to back out.
William wanted to tell them
something ,but they did not hear
his shout.

Across the street was a couple who
kept their home very smart.
In front of their home their
mailbox was a work of art.
The mailbox was sculptured with
grill work in silver.
The mailmen admired it when they
did deliver.

Now Uncle was not the best auto
driver.
He had an impetuous nature,
sometimes a contriver.
He put his car in reverse and
pounded the gas.
The car sped backwards, William
looked aghast.

Uncle smashed into the mailbox
with a direct hit.
William and Myrna were having a
fit.
Then Uncle shifted forward and
sped away
As if he didn't do anything astray.

William and Myrna had to correct
Uncles mistake
By replacing the mailbox, no small
take.
Now, they do not have in their
character, spite,
,but they hoped it wouldn't be
necessary to re-invite.

The Motor Cycle

Brother Henry lived not far from
William and Myrna's home.
One day he decided to take a ride
and come.
The vehicle he used was somewhat
unusual.
He borrowed his daughter's motor
cycle, there was no refusal.

William noted something coming
up the street.
It did not speed nor was it very
discreet.
Henry wanted to show off what he
was driving.
A miniature cycle up the driveway
was arriving.

Henry showed it to William and
Myrna, so proud.
The engine ran well, not too loud.
Henry told William "give it a try",
he insisted.
William said "no thanks" and
graciously resisted.

Henry repeated "there is nothing to
it, just hop on and drive".
William said "no", he wanted to
stay alive.
After numerous requests and
Henry's beguile
William assented and mounted the
cycle.

William put his hands on the
handle bars;
They contained the throttle, not
like cars.
He turned the bars a natural
feeling.
The bike took off like anything
reeling.

He sped across the backyard lawn.
He thought he would reach his
final dawn.
His hands on the bars were frozen
and not free.
He really regretted this stupid
spree.

William was headed toward a
neighbor's tree, the bike was
canted.
It was just a little sprout that was
recently planted.
Myrna asked Henry "Where is he
going?"
Henry was worried, his anxiety
showing.

William decided there was only
one thing to do.
He jumped off the bike and hoped
his life would renew.
The bike also fell and was
churning on its side.
This was not expected, not this
kind of ride.

William survived, a helmet he was
wearing.
He never again wanted this kind of
tearing.
The bike sustained some minor
damage.
That was good considering the
recent rampage.

William returned the bike to Henry
waiting.
Some expletives he said berating.
Henry was laughing and did not
know what to say.
,but William in protest, sent him on
his way.

The Weather Lady

The Northeast is exposed to
weather of all kinds
From sleet, rain, thunder storms
and snow blinds.
Inhabitants are cognizant of the
weather every day.
They listen to TV and radio to
whatever the meteorologists say.

Computer models are used for
prediction.
Many listen intently, it's an
addiction.
Myrna grabbed on to the weather
early.
She became devoted to the reports
without being surly.

William on the other hand didn't
bother very much.
He accepted whatever the weather
brought as such.
He really didn't have to listen to
any predictions.
Myrna would always pass along
the conditions.

One day the couple was slated to
travel.
Myrna heard the weather and
began to unravel.
"We can't go today, there will be
torrential rain".
William disagreed with that
familiar refrain.

"Every time we need to go some
place
We get cancelled by weather to
face".
"The car we bought is all wheel
drive
We can use it in any weather to
survive".

"This part of the country is well
prepared;
Snow removal and emergency
services prevent impair".
"The car has an emergency kit
In case something happens and we
get hit".

William convinced Myrna to take a
chance.
The excursion was delightful,
perhaps she advanced.
William thought he had Myrna
convinced.
,but the next day she reported anew
and William winced.

Myrna kept reporting the weather
every day.
To stop her, there was no way.
She always had the weather ready.
That's why she is the Weather
Lady.

Washing Machine

The washer made noise when it
was spinning.
It did not go away ,but got worse
continuing.
William and Myna had a service
contract.
And so it was time to make the
necessary contact.

The repair man arrived and tested
the machine.
He said the bearings were going
and that could be mean.
Repairs would have to wait service
agency agreement.
If too expensive a buyout was the
appeasement.

After some time the service agency
paid.
Almost full price, "not bad" they
said.
The couple decided to buy new
devices.
They bought the best of the new
contrivances.

A new washer and dryer, both front
loading.
With all kinds of gadgets,
capability exploding.
They waited anxiously for the
machines arrival.
They had a backlog of wash to do
for survival.

The new machines had options
galore,
From cycle, spin, temperature,
there was room for no more.
When the washer turned on lights
beamed everywhere
Like a juke box except no music in
the air.

All the possibilities added to some
six thousand combinations.
Running the machine could be very
frustrating.
Myrna pushed the buttons to
exactly what she desired.
,but she forgot how to start, she
was ready to fire.

The washer had extra load
capacity.
It could handle blankets and quilts
with facility.
That was a feature Myna wanted to
have,
,but she had to be careful; she did
not fall in the cave.

An advertised feature was second
floor spin.
It could be installed there without
causing chagrin.
,but on max spin there was some
vibration.
They were glad it was in the
basement foundation.

Gradually the machines assets
showed.
Clean washes and good drying
caused Myrna to glow.
It's like anything else that takes
getting used to.
Immediate satisfaction is reserved
only for a few.

The Last Move

William and Myrna are getting on
in years.
Their lives have been full, no
regrets and no tears.
,but taking care of a home has
taken its toll.
They needed to look for a different
role.

They had lived in their home, years
totaling thirty one.
The material accumulation could
be a ton.
They put a deposit on a pleasant
senior community.
The work ahead was awesome,
there was no immunity.

They contacted a real estate agent
who could help sell their home.
The price predicted was a shock
down to the bone.
The couple had poured so much
into their palace.
To sell it for cheap does not
provide solace.

The biggest problem facing the
couple
Was proper disposal without
producing rubble.
Downsizing to an apartment was
decided;
Less than half the space the house
had provided

The move required a detailed plan.
It could not be done in the way of
a cram.
William made a layout of the new
living space.
He measured all the furniture in his
present place.

He then inserted furniture into the
plan.
He fit what he could ,but not like a
sardine can.
When he was through, they knew
what they could take;
The rest required disposal, a hard
decision to make.

When the plan was shown to
Myrna, she sat down and cried.
William said "What can we do, we
really tried".
Now that they knew what had to be
disposed.
Methodology became the problem
enclosed.

Can we sell the stuff in an estate
sale?
The thought turned Myrna
decidedly pale.
After due consideration and back
and forth sway.
A tax deduction was available if
they gave it all away.

The house was put up on the
market.
A definite price they had as a
target.
As a matter of convenience, they
were told
Was to move before the house was
sold.

As it came to pass, the new place
was ready.
It was time for final arrangements
and to stay steady.
They hired a mover who did also
pack.
The plan must be executed, no
turning back.

They called the charity
organization to come
And pick up the furniture to be
removed from the home.
The movers came with boxes and
began to pack.
They were quite good, capability
they did not lack.

Notification was made for a new
address.
No reasons were offered, no need
to confess.
When you live so long in one
particular place
Numerous contacts are made with
sincere grace.

Utilities, Doctors, Cable,
Newspaper etc. were all notified.
They made sure their mail was
consigned.
They moved all delicates
themselves.
Many were to be placed on built in
shelves.

They went to the new place to
organize.
When the movers came they
wanted no surprise.
At the new place unpacking began.
Furniture was placed according to
plan.

Contact was made for cable and
internet connection.
The new place provided security
protection.
It took several days ,but peace
finally arrived.
Although exhausted, they did not
feel deprived.

They were also advised their house
had a buyer;
It was a legitimate offer, no flyer.
The home we loved we were glad
to sell.
Life brings big changes; you must
do what makes you feel well.

After a while life settled to routine
contentment.
The couple was happy, there was
no resentment.
This was not exactly the last move
they'd make.
The next would be when god does
his take.

THE VICISSITUDES OF GOLF

Hit the Green

Gordon was a foursome member.
They played every weekend until
September.
Gordon tries ,but he wasn't a good
golfing kind,
,but a nicer guy would be hard to
find

The third hole at the municipal
course
Was a par three, 150 yards, that
could be a lot worse.
A good iron shot could make the
green.
Most in the foursome could make
it clean.

Somehow, Gordon had a tainted
perspective.
On this hole he could not reach the
objective.
The ball was short or either to the
left or right.
Perhaps his trouble was eye sight.

137

Behind the green was a wooded
area.
To be long would be nothing
scarier.
Otherwise the hole was not too
hard
And could provide a par on the
scorecard.

On one sunny Saturday day
It was Gordon's turn to play.
He went into his waggle and lined
up his shot.
He said today he was feeling hot.

The ball took off in a beautiful
flight.
The foursome gazed in surprise at
the sight.
The ball landed in a perfect spot on
the green.
Gordon jumped for joy "see what I
mean".

He received congratulatory
handshakes all around.
Words of good cheer, a most
welcome sound.
This achievement will be
remembered over time
And Gordon will try to remember
his line.

The shot however had a surprise.
A shepherd dog shot out of the
woods to where the ball lied.
He scooped up the ball in his
menacing mouth.
He took off in a flash and headed
south.

Gordon watched the retrieval in
absolute shock.
The dog ruined the day he wanted
to lock.
What's to remember about
Gordon's great shot.
Not Gordon ,but the dog that
destroyed Gordon's pride a lot.

The Shank

It happens in golf, a shot gone
awry.
Often it means, the ball, Good bye.
One type of errant shot that has a
high rank;
It is very unpleasant, it is called a
shank.

A shank occurs when the ball hits
the club all the way inside of
center.
It practically hits where the shaft
enters.
The result is nearly a perpendicular
flight.
The ball goes careening to the
right.

It happened to Walter one golfing
day,
A most embarrassing display.
Not a pleasant sight for everyone
to see,
The ball had landed on a nearby tee

Walter went to retrieve his ball, his
face a red blotch.
Another player on the tee was
dancing around holding his crotch.
Walters face was in a maximum
state of deflate.
"What have I done, did I castrate?"

Walter apologized profusely for
the error.
He was in a state of consternation
and terror.
The dancing victim could no
longer refrain.
He busted out laughing; he was not
really in pain.

Walter sighed heavily in great
relief.
For what he thought he had done
was beyond belief.
The victim took pity on Walter's
demise.
They became good friends,
although hard to surmise.

Golf Etiquette

After work, the golf leagues had
begun.
Employees were happy, there was
some sun.
League rules did not discriminate.
Both men and women could
participate.

Your weekly opponent was a
subject of schedule.
It was something no one could
meddle.
At the course, foursomes were
determined ad-hoc.
You mixed with a variety from the
player stock.

Walt's foursome had hitters that
were long.
The sun was out, a beautiful day,
what could go wrong.
Wade was the longest hitter of the
four.
An accomplished golfer who could
shoot a low score.

The foursome ahead included the
librarian.
Her name was Juanita, sometimes
a contrarian.
Juanita clearly was of South
American descent.
A Carmen Miranda figure with an
excitement bent.

On the eighth hole Walt's
foursome was waiting.
Those ahead of us were on the
green debating.
Who was the furthest from the hole
As he or she would go first as the
rules disclose.

Wade was impatient and decided to
swing.
He didn't think he could reach the
green ring.
The ball went further than he
thought.
It trickled on to the green, a stroke
that was naught.

Juanita turned around and stared at
Walt.
Some Spanish invectives toward
Walt was caught.
He tried to explain that it was not
his hit.
It did not matter, Juanita continued
to spit.

Walt pointed to Wade as the guilty
one.
,but Wade didn't admit to what he
had done.
He shrugged his shoulders and
pleaded not knowing
And Walt no longer could get a
library borrowing.

The Game of Golf

A fun game is the representation.
The reality, a different type of
frustration.
Walt has been playing a long long
time.
If there is any improvement, it's
confined.

He bought books on how to swing.
,but you have to remember more
than one thing.
Left arm straight, full turn on top
Shift weight back and forward,
"Wait, please stop!"

It is impossible to remember all
those things
When you're in the middle of your
swing.
You must reduce to one swing
thought
And hope you don't violate what's
taught.

You best keep your mind clear
And make your swing without fear.
You hope the ball takes proper
flight.
If it does it's a wonderful feeling
and sight.

Perhaps new clubs could make a
difference.
Advertisements say it has
significance.
Some two grand later, a new set of
clubs.
However, on the golf course, the
same flubs.

Some things about golf is
concerning.
Why do golfers keep returning?
All it takes is one good shot.
That's what is remembered, no
matter what.

There are other things of enticing
nature.
Outdoors on the course is an asset
to capture.
Then there is camaraderie with
your friends
As you discuss your scorecard
trends.

Another advantage of golf rage.
You can play until old age.
Longevity is an important desire.
A significant activity after you
retire.

Walt was adamant, he played for
many years.
Some scattered good rounds ,but
mostly tears.
Why continue this unfortunate
progress.
For him to quit, would take an act
of congress.

So he continued to look forward to
every golf day.
With tremendous enthusiasm he
could not sway.
For whatever reason he could not
refrain,
For everything about golf produces
a love of the game.

Language of Golf

Golf is an ancient sport.
Dating back to the 17th century or
sort.
Language was different in the days
of yore,
,but words sustained themselves to
be sure

Let's consider some words like
"caddie".
Who carries clubs today as a
laddie.
The word emanates from the
French "le cadet".
Military boys who served the
royalty set.

How about the warning word
"Fore".
It's used on the golf course galore.
It means "watch out for my ball".
The term is well known to golfer's
all.

"Fore" has several derivations.
A "Fore Caddie" assumed a ball
destination.
To get his attention, the golfer
yelled "Fore".
That's one explanation as
described by lore.

"Beware Before" an old military
warning.
To the front lines to take cover of
projectile storming.
Golfers shortened the term to those
located in advance.
"Watch out, avoid the ball, if you
must dance".

How about Birdie, which is one
under par on a hole.
In olden slang "bird" meant
excellent we are told.
Birdie led to an "Eagle", one stroke
less than "Birdie".
Then an "Albatross", one stroke
less than "Eagle", you see.

A "Bogey" is one over par, a bad
situation.
From the bad "Bogey Man" is the
connotation.
Then there is the word "Dormie"
derived from "Sleep".
A player cannot lose the match, it's
his to keep.

A sand trap is called a "Bunker".
Not a good place to be ,but you
don't hunker.
A "Mulligan is a do-over shot.
Derives from the man who might
have done it a lot.

And so the game retains a language
all its own.
It has survived the years, full
blown.
So use it on the course to maintain
the tradition of the game.
,but you still have to master the
swing to gain any fame.

The Excavation

On Saturday our foursome was
ready
For our weekly outing, the
schedule was steady.
We all teed off and things seemed
normal
As we played each hole, there was
nothing formal.

We reached hole number eight, a
par three.
We had to aim left; on the right
was a tree.
Some construction was noticed
nearby.
A big pit had been dug, we know
not why.

After hitting his ball, Sylvester did
wander.
He went to the pit to consider and
ponder.
At first he examined it from its
periphery
Then he disappeared in the pits
anatomy.

It took quite some time for
Sylvester to emerge.
When he did he must have been in
a mud bath submerged.
Mud was all over his body and
clothes.
Why he went into that pit, nobody
knows.

Sylvester used towels and wiped
himself with vigor.
He could no longer play, he had no
time to linger.
At home he stripped down in his
garage
And hosed himself and his clothes,
it was no mirage.

Out in the course is no time for
exploration
Especially a pit under excavation.
They say that curiosity killed the
cat dead.
Please Sylvester, next time use
your head.

Hole in One

William stood on the tee, six was
the number.
He practiced his swing without
encumber.
The hole was par 3, about 150
yards.
He was hoping a par was in the
cards.

When his turn came, he teed the
ball low.
His practice swing had a good
flow.
He hit the ball with a swing serene.
He was hoping for a landing on the
green.

The ball took flight ever so
precisely.
It hit the ground and rolled so
nicely.
The foursome watched to see
where the ball would stop.
It headed for the cup and
disappeared with a plop.

The foursome started yelling and
jumping around.
One guy went six feet off the
ground.
William did nothing, he just stared
As if this lifetime moment hadn't a
care.

The others yelled "What's wrong
with you boy?"
"You should be jumping up and
down with joy"
William considered his hole in one.
And said "It doesn't compare to
the birth of my son".

When the round was over on the
links
William did his duty with a round
of drinks.
The others kept talking about
William's indifference.
He did not consider it an act of
significance.

William stayed calm without any
pluck.
He knew the stroke was purely
luck.
His composure stayed calm, it was
sustained.
Though he realized it would
probably never happen again

The Cart

Eighteen holes of walking is kind
of tough.
For seniors it can be especially
rough.
Dragging a loaded golf bag makes
matters worse.
A golf cart carries everything, like
a hearse.

Walt and Roger always rode
together.
It worked out well, as long as they
had nice weather.
Walt was the driver and foursome
score keeper.
It became Walt's routine, no one
else, no sleeper.

On one particular hole a hill
descended into a lake.
Walt parked the cart on top and
stepped on the brake.
He then left the cart to go to his
ball.
Roger did the same, which was not
unusual.

As Walt prepared his shot he
looked up with a shock.
The cart was rolling down, it came
out of park.
Walt yelled at Roger to go after the
cart
As he was the closest, so that was
his part.

Roger ran as fast as his legs could
carry.
At the accelerating cart, no time to
tarry.
The cart had to be stopped for
goodness sake
Or else it could be submerged in
the lake.

Roger just about made it in time.
His acrobatics was just fine.
He drove the cart back and gave
Walter a frown.
"You didn't secure the brake, you
clown!"

Walt hit his ball and it made the
green.
He made a good swing, it was
clean.
Roger was puffing in an exhausting
disorder.
He swung and hit his ball in the
water.

The rest of the day brought total
cart silence.
Roger was fuming ,but didn't
resort to violence.
We will play that hole again in
September
And when we do, we will always
remember.

The Outing

The office golf league has an
outing
Once a year at a different course
routing.
It was held at Northeast Greens
this year.
Sylvester was to be the
coordinator, a man of no fear.

Sylvester studied the course layout
in great detail.
He wanted everything covered, he
would not fail.
Paper flags were made for the
holes with a prize.
He enjoyed the work although
harder than he did realize.

On the day of the outing our
foursome was early to arrive.
Sylvester was jumpy ,but very
much alive.
He drove his cart all over the
course
To put out the flags, he was the
source.

The rest of us lounged for quite a
while
Until our tee time we sat and
smiled.
Finally at ten was our time to go
off.
The weather was cloudy and the
ground was soft.

On the first hole there was a small
pond to go over.
Further out the rough was covered
with clover.
Sylvester waggled his club very
hard as he looked to go beyond,
,but he topped the ball and it
landed in the pond.

He did the same thing again to our
surprise.
He was a good golfer, we could not
surmise.
Later he did better because he did
relax.
His anticipation of the outing did
his mind tax.

We reached hole number seven and
the rain began.
Umbrella's came out ,but we
continued the plan.
By hole number nine there was a
major downpour.
We hurried to the clubhouse; we
cared not about the score.

We sat down and had coffee to
wait the rain out.
Sylvester we noticed was in a state
of pout.
"Come on; let's go we must finish
the round"
"We've got to end the outing in a
fitting that's sound".

We looked at Sylvester with
incredulity.
The heck with this outings fidelity.
"If you won't come then I'll go it
alone."
Off Sylvester went to get soaked to
the bone.

About one-half hour later Sylvester
stumbled in.
He was dripping wet and soaked to
the skin.
"Well I tried ,but it's impossible
out there;
Sometimes nature doesn't play
fair".

160

On the way home there was a
continuous growl.
Sylvester was sulking as he sat on
a towel.
He considered the rainout a
cardinal sin,
,but you can't fight the weather,
you'll never win

PHILOSOPHY

Age

"Does anyone know a sage
Who can do something about my
age?
It keeps increasing without a stop.
It won't cease until I drop."

At an early age, I wanted to be
older.
That's when I was much bolder.
Now that my age has advanced
I am not sure I can anymore dance.

My object now is to get younger.
,but my body creeks, it needs to get
stronger.
I would hate to apply artificial
means
Like hair color and Botox, that
would make me scream.

One answer may lie in exercise
However, the regimen must revise.
My body does not easily respond
To the strengthening procedures I
was once fond.

I could try to reenter the bar scene
,but that's an unrealizable dream.
It belonged to a long ago life.
Today it would be vehemently
opposed by my wife.

162

Perhaps a trip to mountain ski
country.
That would return a feeling jaunty.
On second thought I wish to
renege;
There's a very good chance I
would break a leg.

It would be nice if age could have
a Mulligan
So that we could live our life
again.
,but there is no such thing as an age
do over,
What's done is done, there is no
cover.

It's unbelievable how fast the years
have gone.
You look back and ask, "what have
I done?'
Taking inventory disappoints the
amount.
"Can I do more, can we restart the
count?"

The answer is not that complicated.
Being who you aren't is over rated.
Act your age and find some
meaning
And stop all that unnecessary
screaming.

There is a lot you can do no matter
how old.
Don't get senile, get bold.
Take care of yourself, especially
your heart.
And if you play golf, take a cart.

Greener Grass

James said goodbye to his wife.
He was headed to work, a part of
life.
He could walk to the train for his
commute.
Life wasn't easy, there was no
refute.

James had a mortgage with an
adjustable rate.
An increase was expected at an
early date.
The children were growing up fast.
How to pay for college was a
worry to last.

James walked through the park on
the way to the station.
He spotted Fontonoy on a bench in
relaxation.
"That guy is so rich, he doesn't
have worries
He has so much money it's
disgusting", while James scurried.

Roger was on his way to collect
unemployment assistance.
He needed the money just to
maintain existence.
He noted Fontonoy sitting in the
park.
For him, he thought, life was a
lark.

Matilda was out with baby in a
stroller carriage.
Her daily walk, to get her mind off
a difficult marriage.
Matilda and husband had problems
of finance.
They needed a money injection for
a solvent stance.

Along the way she saw Fontonoy
sitting on a bench.
That was enough to make her
stomach wrench.
"That guy has millions, a world
without care
Those people are awful, it just isn't
fair".

Mariano was a storekeeper across
the street.
His food establishment was
stacked so neat.
Business was poor in time of
recession.
He had to lower prices and give
sales concessions.

He noted Fontonoy across the way.
"He has too much money, that's all
I can say".
"The world has some strange
institutions
A man like that lives without
retribution".

It was time for Fortonoy to end his
park sojourn.
He picked up his paper and to
home he returned.
A beautiful day it was, with sun so
bright,
His pondering had shed some light.

At home Fortonoy opened the
drawer.
It was the right time to even the
score.
He removed the pistol and placed it
against his head.
And Fortonoy pulled the trigger
and shot himself dead.

Fortonoy was in a state of deep
depression,
And this tale provides an important
lesson.
Envy by nature can make us
meaner.
It is not a wise quality, the grass is
not greener.

Money

What is it that makes the world go
round?
It has a very familiar sound.
What is our measure of success?
It is something about which we
should care less.

Does it inspire us to do good
deeds?
Not really ,but it does take care of
needs.
Does it fulfill our requirements for
good health?
It could do the opposite, although
its actions are stealth.

To get it everyone has an insatiable
appetite.
At times it makes some do things
that are not right.
Some work hard to obtain its
reward.
Others steal and rob it without any
accord.

The answer is money that comes in
various forms.
Coins and bills are the usual
norms.
Other forms include checks and
cards of credit.
They must be backed by funds you
can debit.

169

Money is used to buy material
things
Like homes and cars and wedding
rings.
The more you have, the more you
can buy.
Some lack enough of it, no matter
how hard they try.

Unfortunately, money is a
necessity.
Without it you face calamity.
No one is sure of its distribution,
,but it is needed to maintain your
constitution.

It is strange how some enjoy
riches.
Some comedians make millions
and leave you in stitches.
Many athletes are paid millions,
it's true.
You might think they spend it all
on tattoos.

In the business world, there are
CEO's.
Who are paid salaries that can your
mind blow.
And actors and performers extract
a big piece of the pie.
That is taken from the available
money supply.

Those who manage our money
have recently failed.
A near depression, everything
derailed.
The good news, it will lead to
some regulation
That is sorely needed to prevent
more frustration.

The titans of Wall Street took us
for a ride.
They will pay the price, they can't
hide.
They and the banks came up with
concoctions
Like derivatives, swaps and other
abominations.

The mortgagees sold adjustable
rates
To everyone in sight, they could
not sate.
They did not invite proper
disclosures,
Rates increased and then many
foreclosures.

,But lo, us ordinary peons don't
despair.
Life isn't always something that's
fair.
,but there is more to life than the
mighty dollar.
So stand up and shout, if necessary
holler.

There is love, marriage and family.
There are some who need us
constantly.
We are surrounded by amazements
of nature
For us to enjoy every day, a
beautiful picture.

What's most important is a happy
life
As much as possible that's free of
strife.
We are blessed with freedom in so
many ways,
,but don't forget to contribute to
your 401-K

Twilight

Time has caught me in a state of
fright.
I'm in a zone called Twilight.
It means I must be grateful for
every day of life.
There is no turning back, I must
accept the plight.

It's a time when I should be
making preparations
To insure I have taken care of my
dearest relations.
Don't leave them stranded in the
dark
If by chance heaven I embark.

What else is there to do that's
required?
Make sure to do it all even though
I'm tired.
Complete a listing of all in the till,
And check with the lawyer about
the will.

Before I gave my life these
thoughts
I enjoyed every day that god had
wrought.
I was healthy and enjoying my
days with my spouse.
Everything was good, no gremlins
did arouse.

To the funeral Parlor, a wise
decision.
Advanced preparation·avoids
derision.
It's a good idea to take action
today
While you're still healthy, for the
funeral pre-pay.

When all is done and all informed,
And family agrees and conforms
Then I'll continue life just as
before
For in Twilight, the sun can shine
for ever more.

Innovation

The global economy has put us in a
bind.
We are not used to this economy
kind.
Labor in many countries is
relatively cheap
Allowing our companies big
profits to reap.

Our labor force has difficulty to
compete.
Is the answer large reductions that
are steep?
That would end up lowering our
standard of living.
There must be better ideas for
someone to be giving.

Our labor force has suffered
layoffs massive.
We must attack the problem and
not be passive.
Government help has caused the
deficit to swell.
We can't be going often to that
well.

We cannot compete under global
economy terms.
Let's stop and do a thinking
sojourn.
The dilemma can be answered with
the following proclamation,
The U.S. can advance by
innovation.

Look at Apple with I-Pod and I-
pad.
High sales of these items make
everyone glad.
Boeing has advanced with
materials composite.
Increased efficiency has resulted in
high order deposits.

Innovation requires added
stimulation.
The way to proceed is increased
education.
Advancement should not be
inhibited by educational costs.
We must increase the student
population without time lost.

And so the problem has a solution.
We can bring it to fruition.
What can enhance the economy of
the nation?
It's innovation, innovation,
innovation!

Opportunity

Ours is the land of opportunity.
That statement needs further
scrutiny.
The sidewalks are not made of
gold.
That's a fable that's very old.

So how does one take
opportunity's invitation?
It's true for everyone in the nation.
First you must not be an education
fool.
Try hard and do your best at
school.

Some immigrants come here for a
better life chance.
They work hard and some make
the advance.
It is quite amazing how they can
get it done
With difficult language barriers to
overcome.

The one constant in achieving lofty
ambition
Is hard work, persistence and
dedication.
Once in a while an opportunity is
offered out of the blue.
It happens rarely and to only a few.

There are times when an
opportunity may be lost.
It's part of life, it's the cost.
Do not despair or feel you have a
lack.
Success often goes to those who
fight back.

And so opportunity is mostly a
personal effort.
It's not an entity that can bring you
comfort.
You must pursue opportunities
with all your heart,
And it helps a lot if you are smart.

Parenting

What's this thing that makes our
heart go wild?
It's when we are lucky to have
produced a child.
The act of doing does not take
much capability
,but the result requires lots of
responsibility.

Welcome mom and dad to the city
of parenthood.
Your independence has been
interrupted for good.
The baby sleeps when he wants
,but not in synch
With your schedule, it is difficult
to link.

Feedings can go on in the middle
of the night.
Take turns in attending; that's only
right.
Although it is difficult. a strong
bond is created
Between parents and child who are
forever related.

The years go by exceedingly fast,
,but hours with offspring's will
forever last.
Now is the time to enter pre-
school.
They are to grow up to be
nobody's fool.

Soon they will enter school
elementary.
Parents must participate and not be
sedentary.
Work with them while doing home
work.
Learning improvement is not a
quirk.

High School can be the most
difficult time.
Peer pressures have to be assessed
and cleverly refined.
If the child does something
considered astray
It's not the teacher's fault; put that
thought away.

College comes faster than one can
imagine.
Career selection; not so easy to
determine.
Let them go to their natural talent.
A mistaken selection can only
bring lament.

Then recycling happens to come
along.
When the child sings the marriage
song.
Then they will make their own
family stand,
And you graduate to parents grand.

The Pendulum

The Pendulum swings left and
right.
It continues its path day and night.
If you stare at it you can be
hypnotized.
It is something to consider, you
must realize.

You may ask "what's that swing
Got to do with anything?"
It is a symbol of life that is
revealing.
Look behind the pendulum and you
will see what it's concealing.

Consider politics with our two
party system.
When one fouls up, the other gets
in.
That's the pendulum swing to the
other side.
It goes on and on, this pendulum
ride.

Some think that wealth is all that
one needs
,but then misfortune strikes and
wealth cannot feed.
Tragedy can thwart a successful
man.
Just think about the Kennedy clan.

If one studies football history,
It's hard to repeat a Super Bowl
victory.
Sometimes a team can be at the top
of the heap,
And come from the bottom with an
outstanding leap.

How often do famous persons in
their prime
Have accidents or sickness that
cause decline?
There are some who act with great
pride
And then disappoint with suicide.

The highway is open in all
directions
And then it is covered with much
congestion.
The economy has had boom
ingestion
,but can falter into deep recession.

Prior to the price of homes
implosion
There was an unsustainable rise, an
explosion.
To buy a home required high
finance disclosure,
And then came the fall with many
foreclosures.

It seems that for every happy
event,
It's countered by some discontent.
Perhaps it is what God has
wrought,
And the pendulum continues back
and forth.

MISCELLANEOUS

Baseball

Baseball has become our national
pastime.
It is played between two
perpendicular lines.
The game captivates us in the
months of summer;
Without it life would be a bummer

The history of Baseball dates back
to the 19th century.
It continued to grow exponentially.
Curiosity surrounded its great
actors.
Home runs and no hitters were
some of the factors.

Baseball has not been scandal free,
And they have been divulged for
the world to see.
In 1919 The Chicago black sox
threw the World Series
To obtain gambling money, it
made everyone leery.

Even though the game had some
contraction,
It never really lost its attraction.
Babe Ruth became the king of
swat.
When he swung the bat, he was
always hot.

A catastrophe to the Red Sox team
Was to trade Babe Ruth to the
Yankees, a nightmare dream.
He hit 60 home runs and it is
claimed,
Because of him, they built the
Yankee Stadium.

For a long long time baseball was
exclusionary.
All men were not equal to the
owner visionaries.
That was too bad because some
great players were excluded.
Bias and discrimination were still
rooted.

It was the Brooklyn dodgers under
Branch Rickey
Who took the step that was indeed
tricky.
He signed Jackie Robinson to a
major league contract,
And the floodgates were opened to
all, a significant fact.

Things progressed, everything OK,
Although there is one thing I
would like to say.
A disappointing event occurred
along the way,
When the Brooklyn dodgers
moved to LA

In the 1970's owners lost the right
To keep reins on players and hold
them tight.
Free agency arrived in all its glory
The players were free and they
became the story.

They could demand lucrative
contracts.
Agents were hired so negotiations
would not detract.
Players won the right to contractual
freedom.
But the rich teams hired the best to
feed on.

The game continued its popular
appeal.
New stadiums were built with
services surreal.
One feature of many new parks
construction
Was artificial turf that produced a
game reduction.

Some balls zipped through the
ground.
A high bounce took forever to
come down.
The turf allowed too many hits to
be cheap.
That innovation was not a forward
leap.

Seems like the game was not
scandal devoid.
When some of the players resorted
to steroids.
Some records were broken because
of artificial strength.
No explanation was truthful, no
matter what the length.

The steroid man will not get away
with that trick.
Their record breaking feats will
have an asterisk.
They will all be found out and
identified by name.
It is very doubtful; they will reach
the Hall of Fame.

Salaries and new stadiums have
made the game an expensive
proposition.
,but the crowds keep coming
without diminution.
One hundred dollars per is not
unusual.
So watch it on TV and be casual.

No matter what the game will
survive.
It's popular for fans to dive.
So if by chance you have the time
and money then embark.
Go to a game, the enjoyment is not
a lark.

Computers

In days of yore, we learned at
school
How to use a slide rule
Computations could be very
tedious
Including those that were very
serious.

Then the electronic calculator came
along
I was so happy, I could sing a
song.
It did everything from logs to
trigonometry.
It could even be programmed for
all kinds of geometry.

The early computers were big and
grotesque.
They could not fit on top or under
a desk.
They had to be fed with cards that
were punched.
They were time consuming, no
time for lunch.

Computers were large of very big
size.
There could only be one each
company could realize.
You hoped your user request was
not refused.
Your work required a computer to
use.

I can remember working all night.
To get on a central computer, it
was a fight.
One input mistake and the program
crashed.
Back to the drawing board, the
whole night was smashed.

Then came the invention of miracle
chips.
Computers were cut down to size,
that's not a quip.
They could fit on your desk as a
personal PC.
You had infinite access as far as
you could see.

Productivity leapfrogged that of
the past.
A beautiful feeling that you know
would last.
Commercial programs came into
being and multiplied.
The computer became a necessary
friend at your side.

If you need some help to get
information.
That's no problem, no need to
ration.
Just ask your computer, please find
this data.
And Google will get it sooner than
later.

A computer unfortunately does not
live forever.
It can become obsolete or die
during a computation endeavor.
But in most situations, it acts very
much alive.
Except when your heart sinks and
you lose your hard drive.

In Star Wars there was a computer
named Hal;
To the astronauts an amicable pal.
Like a loved one, the computer
resembles
The greatest tool man has ever
assembled.

Four Seasons

In the Northeast there are four
seasons.
That's just true, no given reasons.
There is winter, spring, summer
and fall;
Some people feel they have it all.

Winters are cold and can make you
feel low.
A Nor Easter brings wind and
snow.
Townships send plows to clear the
routes
Of school buses, for kids they tout.

Bring out the winter clothes to
keep you warm
From the storage closets, that is the
norm.
And if you need a new jacket as
seen,
You can always send away to L.L.
Bean.

Snow blowers and shovels come
out and abound.
Several feet of snow can astound.
But the world doesn't stop because
of the weather.
In the Northeast, they have got it
together.

To some the winter brings a
multitude of sports.
Like skiing, hockey, skating of
sorts.
Others cut holes for fishing in the
ice.
It's a way to have fun at any price.

In winter the trees are bare and
daylight short.
You must use lots of heat for
needed comfort.
It's welcome when the thaw melts
the snow,
And when you see a robin, then
spring begins to show.

The trees begin to bud and the
grass turns green.
Yard cleanup is necessary to
ensure it is clean.
The golf clubs can come out of the
basement.
The winter has crimped your swing
in amazement.

When spring approaches its full
bloom.
You must plant flowers and the
grass to groom.
Take out the lawn mower and
change its oil.
Make sure the controls are
adjusted, it takes some toil.

Place the winter clothing in the
closets of storage.
Bring out the lighter clothing, and
enjoy the spring foliage.
Start mowing the lawn and
applying weed control.
Check the weed whacker and edger
and fill your petrol.

Look at the trees and see what has
to be pruned.
It's important to do so before
branches are ruined.
The time has come to apply initial
fertilizer.
Crab grass and Weed control are
the required sterilizers.

Soon the trees are in full bloom
Filled with heavy leaves to groom.
We must call the landscaper to
apply the spray,
To keep the bugs and disease
away.

Then summer approaches and
more of the same.
Only the temperature is hotter,
sweat is hard to contain.
The bushes have grown and need
to be trimmed.
Out comes the trimmer and saw for
loose limbs.

Prior to the summer months in full
swing,
There is some more effort on an
important thing.
To keep the house cool under
temperatures that gets hot,
The air conditioning must be
serviced before it is used a lot.

The grass on the lawn protrudes
over the driveway edge.
The edger is used to produce a nice
ledge.
Keep watching the grass for any
discolor.
Apply more fertilizer to keep the
grass fuller.

As the summer drags on and we
engage in summer sports.
Look around and everyone is
wearing shorts.
It's a pleasant time of the year to
travel around.
The Northeast sights are great and
their numbers abound.

When the summer fades and we
approach the fall,
Leaves begin to drop from trees
tall and small.
Leaves change color to provide a
glorious view.
They come from near and far to
taste nature's menu.

Although the leaves provide a
beautiful picture,
They demand a price without any
lecture.
Leaves must be assembled and
properly disposed.
It is not easy work as my muscles
disclose.

You cannot stop time, deny or
abstain.
Winter returns with its cold refrain.
Four seasons require work that can
pile
,but nature's bounty makes it all
worthwhile.

Grid Lock

What gives with our law-making
bodies?
Nothing gets done, a bunch of
stodgies.
We have mostly a two party
system
,but neither to the people, do they
listen.

Considerable time is spent on
campaigns
In which, each other, they defame.
They each tell us everything they
want to do.
After election, nothing gets done,
maybe a few.

The two law making bodies are the
house and senate.
They are there by the voter's
consent.
The two parties are Republicans
and Democrats.
Each acts like a bunch of
aristocrats.

The house and senate must agree to
make law.
Then the president must supply his
signature
The inter party squabbling is a big
obstacle;
You wonder if anything is
possible.

If our fore fathers knew what was
occurring,
They would get angry at the
politician's slurrying.
They would say, sometimes you
have to fight
,but by golly, get together and do
what's right.

They must explain to the people
without relaxation.
You can't have services without
taxation.
Education is the source of our
success,
It should not be so expensive to
cause duress.

Why can't everyone have decent
health care?
Legislators have it, but they won't
share.
Are we slaves to the insurance
industry?
Premiums will rise, just wait and
see.

It's unbelievable, no words can
define,
A policy to reduce taxes during
war time.
The economy is facing
strangulation,
Because of refusal to apply
regulation.

Our failure to pay has caused
deficits massive.
Nothing is done to correct, they are
passive.
We must get hold of this situation
with determination
And pay the piper his
remuneration.

The system is far from being solid
as a rock.
Too often, we are faced with
gridlock.
They should stop thinking of
themselves and being so feeble.
And start doing something for
constituents, the people.

Hair Dresser

It happens once every week.
Same time and place she seeks.
She wants to look so fair,
So she operates on her hair.

Only one place will she go.
Only one stylist does she want to
know.
Sometimes it's for a wash and set,
And once a month a color rinse she
gets.

The parlor is a busy place.
Women march in to enhance their
face.
From perms to sets and also
bleaching,
The services are far reaching.

Hair dressing goes back a long
long way.
It's amazing how women's
customs stay and stay.
It goes on and on without reprieve;
It might go back to Adam and Eve.

A case can be made that it's a
women's religion
To regularly see her hair
beautician.
The economy also adds to the
situation.

Working women increases the
population.

They must attend no matter what
the weather.
Without it they can't get their act
together.
So it must be accepted, it cannot be
lesser.
They must make their appointment
with the hair dresser.

After the appointment is done,
Then a protective mode is begun.
To go out in weather that is not
fair,
"It's not allowed, it could muss my
hair".

My Insulin Pump

It was easy to predict
That I would become a diabetic.
My mother's family all had the
disease.
It was fatal to some, no way to
ease.

It struck me when I was older.
In my forties, it became bolder.
I started out by taking pills
To combat the pancreatic ills.

I soon advanced to syringes,
An experience that caused cringes.
It was finally recommended that I
take the jump,
And graduate to the insulin pump.

The pump provides painless insulin
delivery,
And it does it continuously.
Before a meal you must add more.
It is called a Bolus, and the pump
keeps score.

The continuous supply is called the
Basal rate.
It can be regulated early or late.
When the insulin supply comes to
conclusion,
You must renew by body infusion.

To know where your blood sugar
stands,
You must test your blood by
pricking your hands.
The blood transfers to a strip and
meter
That reads out your blood sugar,
what could be neater?

The pump provides excellent blood
sugar control,
You might call the system, the
diabetic patrol.
Every three days requires a new
penetration
Of an infusion set with a different
body destination.

The pump is quite small and can be
worn on a belt,
It doesn't interfere, it is hardly felt.
I can still do whatever I desire.
The pump continues to go and does
not retire.

Advances in progress will simulate
the pancreatic condition.
To supply the right amount of
insulin when needed, a neat
rendition.
The pump continues through
serenity and strife.
It has been a Godsend and is
saving my life.

204

Sports

We Americans are enamored with
sports;
We love almost every type of all
sorts.
Even though it is expensive to be a
live spectator,
The stands can usually be filled
early or later..

Let's start in the spring with the
baseball season
Basketball is still going on, no
rhyme or reason.
And the winter sport of hockey
gets ready for playoffs.
Each sport is independent, no
tradeoffs.

Golf is in full swing with the early
majors.
Pro Basketball continues with
highly paid cagers.
Soccer is strong although
popularity has not caught on.
And bowling continues the athletic
song.

The warm weather brings track and
field in the fold.
Then, there's diving and swimming
to behold.
These sports continue the
overlapping schedule.
The organizers don't care, don't
meddle.

In the middle of the summer
football begins.
It's getting confusing, not funny,
no grins.
Then in the fall baseball should be
over
,but the World Series stretches
without cover.

We haven't mentioned NASCAR
races,
And the horses are going through
their paces.
Then the playoffs have started in
the NBA,
And football is going both night
and day.

It's not only professionals that take
their fling.
College teams can also pack them
in.
The TV screen can take a toll on
the eyes
,but the Super Bowl may produce a
surprise.

Now its baseball, football,
basketball and hockey,
And the triple crown for some
famous jockey.
Without all those sports, what
would we do?
The rest of TV produces good
programs that are only a few.

In September tennis is the rage
With the U.S. Open on stage.
Both men and women vie for the
best
As they smack balls across the net.

Every four years Olympic Games
begin.
Both winter and summer they play
to win.
Its country vs. country, all very
serious rage.
Opening and closing ceremonies
spectacularly staged.

March madness arrives, the
elimination begins.
If your favorite team loses it brings
on chagrins.
The cycle restarts with the baseball
season.
All the fans are ready with
determined reason.

We could not live without the
games.
We look for the superstars to make
their fame.
Sports are ingrained in the USA
life.
Without we'd be bored and have
too much strife.

Besides the games producing
entertainment fare,
Many sponsors and advertisers sell
their wares.
Involved are billions of dollars
being spent.
To view sports the wives do
concede and allow their consent.

The Credit Card Caper

Juan received a mail invitation.
It did not require a donation.
It was a credit card application,
Which Juan completed, no
procrastination.

He then used the card to buy
material things.
He was considering taking a fling.
After a month a bill was sent.
Juan paid the minimum because he
still had rent.

Juan did not realize what he was
paying.
Usurious interest applied if full
payment delaying.
He used the card and accumulated
debt.
Minimum payment continued, he
did not forget.

To Juan's surprise another
invitation came in the mail
For a different credit card, Juan's
idea could not fail.
He would use the new card and pay
minimum fee
Until his debt maxed out
gloriously.

Juan received five more
invitations.
Each time he filed the same
information.
He would accumulate material by
the yard,
And pay minimum fee with each
card.

Juan's debt was now reaching
major proportions;
What could he do without getting
contortions?
He decided to continue the process
until they inquired.
There was no easy way to
accomplish debt retired.

They came after Juan with serious
intention.
How will he pay or will he require
detention?
But Juan was not available, where
did he go?
Juan completed his plans to flee to
Mexico.

Now who is to blame for this bad
situation?
Juan certainly contributed with his
infatuation.
But the companies that gave him
the credit cards
Are the primary culprits, they must
be retards.

The GPS

GPS stands for Global Positioning
System.
If you are driving it requires that
you listen.
It can provide directions anywhere
you want to go,
No matter if you are going fast or
slow.

It comes with a windshield
attachment device
And an electrical connection to
auto plug, very nice.
You program the destination
address
And it provides oral directions
without distress.

Directions are given with a
pleasant female voice.
No man would argue with the
choice.
Also, the device provides a map to
view
To further prevent going askew.

Sometimes you know a shortcut
with mileage less
That can be in conflict with the
GPS.
"Recalculating", she announces
with authority
As if you violated her direction
priority.

Whenever you leave the
automobile
You must remove the installation
and conceal.
They are a favorite device for
burglar invaders.
We need more law enforcement
crusaders.

It's amazing, this thing guided by
satellite;
It removes a sad feeling of fright.
It's not overly expensive, a
reasonable cost.
A wonderful feeling that you won't
get lost.

Touch tone

In an era of technology automation
We have become a push button
nation.
A phone call requires digital agility
and care.
You must push the buttons to get
anywhere.

Decide between English or Spanish
lingo.
Then press button 1 or 2 to
continue to go.
Listen carefully because the menu
has changed,
Just adds to confusion, a system
deranged.

If you have a claim, do you know
the number?
If you don't, that's a bummer.
Punch in the number and then the
pound sign.
The procedure is rigid, that's by
design.

If you make a mistake and cannot
complete
There are ways for the system to
repeat.
Press a button for the original
menu
Over again with the starting venue.

If you have done everything right
There may be some daylight in
sight.
The next instruction is hard to
believe
Calls are taken in the order
received.

You must listen to music soft and
fine,
Trying to make people feel
sublime.
Until someone finally responds on
the phone.
By this time you are exhausted and
prone.

To solve your problem you must
redial
To another number that has your
file.
Then the procedure starts again,
English or Spanish, the opening
refrain.

Made in the USA
Columbia, SC
26 July 2017